IRRESISTIBLE

Wifestyles

*Nourishing, Enriching,
& Building
Your Marriage*

Linda Andersen

ACCENT BOOKS
Denver, Colorado

ACCENT BOOKS
A division of Accent Publications, Inc.
12100 West Sixth Avenue
P.O. Box 15337
Denver, Colorado 80215

Copyright © 1990 Accent Publications, Inc.
Printed in the United States of America

Library of Congress Catalog Card Number 89-82608

ISBN 0-89636-258-2

Dedicated to Roy,
my husband,
who has kept me laughing,
loving, and learning.

"A promise made, a promise witnessed, a promise heard, remembered, and trusted—this is the groundwork of marriage. Whether we know it or not, it is a divine thing we do, and it is holy."

Walter Wangerin
As For Me And My House
(Used with permission)

Prologue

This book enters the topsy-turvy world of you, the married woman. It peeps inside your kitchen, your living room, your heart. It looks at some things that work in marriage and some things that don't.

I'm going to share some insights and some very real personal experiences. I'm going to take a walk with you, and do some talking about irresistible wifery, without pretending to answer all or even most of the questions about being a wife. I hope the book will encourage you to allow God to develop attitudes that will make your marriage a lot more enjoyable—more like it was planned to be by God Himself.

The book is directed to the believing wife whether or not she has a believing husband, because biblical principles are a flavor enhancer to *any* marriage.

For over twenty-eight years I have been learning, experimenting, and growing into a fuller understanding of what it is to be a better "half"—a "suitable helper" as Genesis 2:18 says.

Like you, I am a wife. I am also a mother, a neighbor, a wage earner (at times), a daughter, a niece, an aunt, and the list goes on. But over and above them all, I am a child of God and then a wife, in that order.

By the grace of God, Roy and I have a relationship that dances—that moves with the currents of time and still keeps tune. For that I humbly thank our God. I don't know what's ahead, but each new day is a fresh chance to walk with the Spirit, and to accept or reject the perfect wisdom found in God's Word.

This isn't meant to be a book of burdens, or do's and don'ts, but, rather, one that opens new doors of freedom to new ways to *enjoy* married happiness. I pray that each precept will be a key to unlock happy new adventures in marriages.

I gladly open the doors of my experience and point to the power and presence of the living Christ as the most vital ingredient in any marriage that wants to stay in tune.

Step with me into a hallway of mirrors—where we can look at ourselves, our mates, and our God.

Part 1

Woman, wife, and helpmate. Rediscovering femininity and womanliness in God's design.

— 1 —
Child Of God—
Wife Of Man

There's no way around it. We marry men, not perfect beings. We marry men with peanut butter on their faces and pants that need hemming. Be they ever so lovable, they're totally man—and totally human. And they are a perfect match for woman.

Even a newlywed discovers tarnish on her angel's wings soon enough. If he appears god-like at times, love has covered a multitude of imperfections (thank goodness!). But even love sees clearly at times and must admit that the human object of its devotion is ever so human—ever so fallible.

From the beginning of time, a woman's love for a man has been and is the most natural thing in the world. It was one of the first needs God fulfilled for humans. And, after all, God created men and women for each other. "It is not good for the man to be alone," God said in Genesis 2:18. Need meets need, and the two become one. And, it's good, as it was planned to be . . .at least a lot of the time.

But good can turn sour when we start expecting our man to be God. If we expect a husband to meet *all* of our needs, we're in for a disappointment. He won't, and he can't. Meeting needs completely is a function of God alone. A wife needs to recognize that early in marriage (and preferably *before*!) because a lot hinges on it. If we recognize God as the only perfect supplier of our soul, our feelings, our emotions, our well-being, anything our husband does will be a wonderful extra.

If we turn a wife's needs inside out, we have a husband's needs. Husbands need a lot from their wives whether or not they verbalize it. And when a wife begins to focus on making her husband's life enjoyable, a surprising process begins down deep inside her, transforming her from a dissatisfied *taker* into a satisfied *giver*. By giving we receive (Luke 6:38). A wife who is not continually focused on *her* needs opens the door to genuine marital satisfaction. If you have not read a sentence like this in a long time, it's because they are in short supply. But then. . .so are marriages that last.

God did not create doormats. He created "completers, helpmates." A woman who is growing in the Lord *will* increase her capacity to be unselfish and her ability to look for meaningful ways to express love to her husband. "For it is God who is at work in you, both to will and to work for His good pleasure" (Philippians 2:13). When the husband is committed to following Christ in this way, also, the home truly becomes an island of joy, a place of refuge.

But this is a book about *wife*styles, the wife's responsibility before the Lord to honor the commitment she made on her wedding day. We can't change anyone else. We must look within ourselves for areas that need God's cleansing, straightening, soothing hand. This isn't a book about a husband's responsibility before the Lord. It's far more personal. . .and may hurt as we look at life beyond the outraged cry, "But he didn't do. . . ." "But he isn't the right kind of husband. . . ."

He may not have and he may not be. But that doesn't lessen *our* responsibilities.

Then, too, we must allow our husbands to fail. They'll do it anyway because they *are* husbands and humans. But failure is a marvelous teacher—one of the best. To allow our mate to fail, secure in the safety net of our continuing love and trust, is to free him to mature. It is also to trust *God* to work in his life. Communication and trust are the keys—together with keeping our hearts pure before the Lord.

We need to share our insights when decisions are being made, but there is a time to step back and be a cheerleader when he decides firmly in some direction. Yes, there will be times when a wife will suffer because of poor decisions. But when we see those times as part of God's plan to make us more Christ-like, we give ourselves opportunities to grow. God is, after all, more committed to conforming us to Christ than to making us more comfortable. He allows exactly what it takes to refine us and create a rich patina of Christian maturity. Sometimes, failure, not success, is what it takes.

We are children of God. He's our Father. Each day is a fresh start as we ask Him to teach us to love our husbands *as they are*. . .very human children of a God who is committed to the character development of both partners. Our expectations need to be realistic, yet we can encourage our husbands to rise to their full potential (without nagging!) by our trust in them—and in the sovereignty of the Lord Jesus Christ.

Not gods? No, our husbands are not all-knowing, superhuman creatures. They *are* warm, wonderful, funny, and exasperating human beings with a God who invented marriage and who wants to take charge

11

of his life and ours. Our God stands, now and always, ready to assume responsibility for our lives (Romans 12:1-2) and the consequences of our obedience.

Take another look at your husband. He *is* the man you chose above all others to receive your love. He *is* worthy of your loving efforts to make his life as pleasant a journey as possible.

Stop for a few moments and remember. Remember *why* you chose him. Remember why he chose you. Remember the way it was. And know in your heart that *today* you can make it feel like that again.

Biblical Principle:
   The *greatest* quality is love.

My Scripture:
   "[Love] does not seek its own, is not provoked, does not take into account a wrong suffered" (I Corinthians 13:5).
   "Thanks be to God that. . .you became obedient from the heart to that form of teaching to which you were committed" (Romans 6:16).
   ". . .Let each of you regard one another as more important than himself" (Philippians 2:3).

My Prayer:
   "God of my life, help me focus on making my husband's life enjoyable in a special way today. Help me truly consider him and his needs as more important than me and mine. Take this dissatisfaction away and transform it as only you can. Give me the capacity to be unselfish—one day at a time. Help me remember the good times. . .and let today be a new beginning. I love you, Lord."

— 2 —
You've Got What It Takes

There are all kinds of ways we wives sort of fill in the empty corners of our husband's life—ways we put a sparkle in his eyes and a bounce in his steps. And the nice part of it is, we often do it without even trying, just because we're women.

Way back in the beginning of time, God adorned woman with a stunning array of the very feminine qualities our "Adams" would need. This is not to say He created us as good housekeepers or even mothers, but that He poured into woman, into us, the natural ability to "complete" or round out a husband's life experience.

When God reached down into Adam and made Eve out of his rib, He made a creature who had the ability to flesh out the human experience of Adam, her husband. She was a distinctive and complete creation —a co-regent with Adam over their world. In one lightning stroke of creation, God brought to Adam one he could snuggle up to in both body and spirit— because the Garden of Eden and the animals didn't quite do it. When God said, "It is not good for the man to be alone; I will make him a helper suitable for him"

(Genesis 2:18), He was telling us that man needs a woman, a completer—the other half of him.

So what does this "completing" mean to you? For one thing, it means that you, as Eve's direct descendant, already have the basic tools to become a satisfying mate. You are able to become the soul mate he *needs* whether or not he is even aware he needs it.

Husbands and wives don't often stop to articulate just "why" we are drawn to marry each other. But mixed into all the reasons you may have for marrying *him* is a basic *need* for his kind of male companionship. And mixed into *his* bag of reasons for choosing you is a need he may not even be aware of for a "completer." They need what we have. Otherwise, our husbands could marry trees!

Be glad for the natural, God-given abilities you have. Be glad you are needed. If he *seems* not to need you, it may only be that other activities have, for the time being, captured his energies and he hasn't taken the time to think about it.

More than one marriage, loving in the beginning, has come crashing to earth with the speed of light when the wife can bear the loneliness no more. His work devours him and spits out the crumbs on her doorstep. But crumbs aren't enough. And when it's over, he's left a broken man, with a million dollars in his hands and children who barely know him. Only then do some stop to realize it is *her, them* he needs. And then, it is too late.

A woman begins with inborn abilities to "complete" a husband. As we grow in Christ, the power of the Spirit of God polishes character qualities produced by Him so that our marriages and our lives will flourish into a garden of vibrant colors.

Completer—missing link—able helper—that's you

and me. What a wonderful package God has put together! We're bursting with possibilities and potential! We're the sunrise half of marriage, the rainbow side of a dazzling duet!

So what are some of the qualities about us that "complete" our husbands? What about us fleshes out his bones and makes him stand inches taller and smile a lot bigger? You may have other things to add on a list of your own. Here are mine.

- Our very femininity.
- Our innate sense of grace and beauty.
- Our sensitivity.
- Our softness.
- Our warmth.
- Our special capacity for devotion.
- Our depth of understanding.
- Our lady-likeness (a forgotten word!).
- Our life fragrance as we surrender to Christ.

And this is only a small basketful of the fruits poured into woman—into us. We have a head start on becoming a satisfying (maybe even an *exhilarating*) wife by virtue of our created natures.

Then comes the question of whether our husbands are to get the benefit of *all* our "fruits." Certainly they don't *deserve* them all the time—or do they? Your husband and mine are the men we have pledged our lives to in a promise before God and man. He is the one we chose above all others in the world to intertwine our lives with. Who better to receive our "first-fruits"? Who better to get the significant portion of our interest and our energies? Children will grow up and leave home. They are not pledged to live with us the rest of their lives (and they shouldn't!). Our husband is. Long after the nest is emptied, we will be together in a relationship woven of years. If we are to enjoy those years, we must invest our "firstfruits" regularly.

The God-given feminine qualities we possess have a supernatural way of transforming a husband, over time, into the best person he can become. We dare not spend our days giving *all* of our energies and time to others. If we leave our husbands only the peelings and core of our life, he will get tired of leftovers. He'll starve to death before we realize he's hungry. Or he might look elsewhere to nourish his manliness.

There are choices for us to make every day in this regard. Personal goals or mutual goals? A solo or a duet? Two separate highways or a trip together through life with a lot of special moments along the way? Our husbands? Or _____.

Where marriage is concerned, it just might be time for a revolution which could be long overdue. It may be time to pull back, regroup, rethink, replan, replenish, refurbish, and remake our marriages *God's* way.

If Christian wifestyles *are* radical, even foolish and laughable to unbelievers, so be it. The time is *now* to hunger and thirst after God's ways; to take Him up on His promises and live like *believers.* Our challenge is to ask God to make us thirst for His best.

Titus 2:4–5 tells us that wives are to, ". . .encourage the young women to love their husbands, to love their children, to be sensible, pure, workers at home, kind, being subject to their own husbands, that the Word of God may not be dishonored." Now *that's* radical!

Married happiness is on God's agenda for us. He wants it. He designed it. Our God isn't out to take away our toys. Rather, He stands, arms extended, to assist us, love us, help us. But we have choices to make. His way or ours. Rebellion or obedience. Self-centeredness or other-centeredness. Let's give God the authority that's rightfully His to replenish and renew our hearts—to stimulate and encourage us. Let's ask Him to give us a mental picture of who we are as wives and what we can do to produce a satisfying marriage by His grace. It could be the beginning of some bright surprises!

Biblical Principle:
Husbands and wives naturally complement each other.

My Scripture:
"But for Adam there was not found a helper suitable for him. So the Lord God caused a deep sleep to fall upon the man, and he slept. Then He took one of his ribs and closed up the flesh at that place. And the Lord God fashioned into a woman the rib which He had taken from the man, and brought her to the man" (Genesis 2:20–22).

My Prayer:
"Suddenly I feel *special*, Lord. Your Word tells me who I am and what I do best. What a freedom I have in this! I think I've been a little like a swan behaving like an alligator. Show me how to fully enjoy this freedom of being a woman and teach me today how I can 'complete' my husband best."

Gratefully yours,

— 3 —
Off The Pedestal

Mother Eve really had an awful lot going for her didn't she? She had a perfect, sinless husband, a flawless garden home, plenty of "space" (a whole globe of it!), sparkling, environmentally pure rivers and lakes, no crime, no perversion, no sickness, no drugs, and no abuse. She didn't even have a sinful past to choke her up with bad memories.

And then Adam and Eve chose. By their decision to sin against their Creator, they tinted their world and ours a sad shade of Forever Blue.

You and I no longer marry perfect men. The man you married, the husband I love, each is subject to *all* the frailties of our fallen race. Your husband *will* sin. He *will* disappoint you. He *will* fail you. He *will* be quick tempered and shortsighted and unthoughtful and even unkind at times. He may be cutting and critical, bruising your spirit. None of these are good, and none are necessary, but they may be real experiences in your marriage at different times.

Stop for a minute and take an objective look at your husband: Who is he and who do you expect him to be? Are they two different people? Is your husband the unwitting slave (or target) of your expectations? Have you got him on a pedestal of your making? How long has he been there? It's uncomfortable up there, you know. He *knows* he cannot meet all of your expectations. Sometimes he's too tired or frustrated to try anymore.

Do you have a private, unwritten agenda for him to follow? You know a list of things "a good Christian husband" *ought* to do? Take it out and look at it. Where did you get those criteria? Books? The radio? Television? When did you begin your list and why do you keep adding to it?

If you do have a hidden agenda for your husband, *he knows it.* He will instinctively know he is not quite a match for *any* situation (in the estimation of the one person he chose to spend his life with), and he may begin a male retreat: silence, work, a newspaper, TV.

If you find yourself in a guilty blush on any of these counts, you are not alone. Rare is the woman who has *no* unrealistic expectations for her husband. But if your agenda *dominates* your relationship and dictates your conversations and infects your marriage, STOP! Remember, plainly and clearly, that you married a man, not a perfect being.

There's no way around it. You married a man who forgets your birthday; a man who loses his keys and his temper with equal regularity. You may even have discovered the rough edges on your angel's tongue as early as the honeymoon or as late as yesterday. Be he ever so lovable, he's totally and unmistakably human (just like you!).

Our problem usually comes because we want compassion, consideration, and concern from him, for us, consistently, and first. We want to receive it, and it's hard to give when it isn't reciprocated. Thankfully,

God sees, rewards, and wants us to obey Him—even if it's tough.

Marriage *can* be a good and happy thing for us, but it will never be perfect. Neither will a husband. Perfection will come only in eternity, so for now, our feet are firmly planted in the everyday realities of *our* imperfections *and* those of our husbands!

Not only is a husband not perfect, he is needy. When we begin to focus on discovering his needs and how to fulfill them, we open the door to marital joy.

Wives are partners in the adventure called marriage, but we need to be prepared for some failures along the way. Sometimes seeming success is really failure because of the neglected relationships left in its wake. And sometimes failure is really success because a man has done his very best. That's when we trust in God's sovereignty, confident that He is still in charge.

Put your hand (and *your* needs!) in the hand of God. Ask Him to help you love your husband as he is. . .a very human child of an all-wise God who brought you together and is committed to the character development of both of you. Keep your expectations realistic, yet be your husband's biggest fan club.

Biblical Principle:
   Only God can meet all my needs (I Peter 5:7).

My Scripture:
   "And my God shall supply all your needs according to His riches in glory in Christ Jesus" (Philippians 4:19).

My Prayer:
   "God of my life, help me focus on making our

marriage fun in a special way today. Take this dissatisfaction away and transform it as only you can. Give me the capacity to be unselfish—one day at a time. Bring back memories of all the good times. And let today be our new beginning."

— 4 —
Men Will Be Men

It has been a long time since men and women were created, but despite Genesis 1 and 2 and cutting edge technology, some still insist that men and women are exactly alike, or at least that there's no significant difference. I wonder why?

To me, the differences are wonderful as well as exasperating, but there *are* obvious differences.

I've spend a lot of years observing fathers, brothers, uncles, grandpas, and friends, not to mention a husband. If there is *anything* true about our male counterparts, it is this: They are decidedly (and often delightfully) different from us.

Let's look briefly at the differences which seem to be the hardest for couples to reconcile. The physical, the emotional, and the social.

The most obvious difference is physical. Few would challenge the fact that most men are created with a more muscular skeleton. They have a frame built to take more physical punishment than a woman's frame. What this means to a wife is several things.

First, there are definite benefits in having a husband who is stronger than you are. There is work he can do that a wife doesn't have to worry about. A man is constructed to do heavy work and compete in physically grueling sports without undue harm. Heavy work is more of a challenge to a woman's frame, and common sense needs to be exercised if heavy work is involved in her choices in order not to suffer needlessly.

One day I watched a woman who was about 50-years-old lift shovelsful of rocks for her landscaping project, and wondered *when* she would pay, not *if.* There may be cases where this kind of work simply can't be avoided, but if it can, why take unnecessary risks with your health?

Some assume these risks to "make a statment," and for some I know, it has cost them the joy of childbearing or other extended problems. I've "made a statement" myself and paid a high price both in doctor visits and time wasted as well as in discomfort. To keep in shape is to be a good steward of your body, but competition for the sake of proving ourselves to be something we are not built to be is another thing.

I believe the wise, godly wife will focus more on admiring her husband's physical prowess than competing with it. It is possible to challenge our husbands to the extent that we filter off their enjoyment of their own strength and masculinity. They *enjoy* doing some things better than we can, just as we enjoy doing some things they simply cannot. When we delight in the distinctiveness of being a woman, it allows our husbands to enjoy the distinctiveness of being a man.

Stronger is not *better*. Stronger is *different*. Men and women are two different beings with different kinds of strengths. Each is absolutely necessary and neither is superior. To believe either of you are inferior in any way is to walk right past who each of you are in Christ without really seeing your personal value.

A man enjoys his strength and his manliness. And

he hopes you will recognize it and enjoy it, too. Men have little opportunity to display and enjoy their physical strength due to the offices and chairs which are now part of the "work" of so many. He needs *someone* he can count on to recognize and appreciate that uniqueness.

God did not create husbands and wives to compete with each other, but to complement and enjoy each other. When we use our energies to play "catch up" or "I'm as tough as you," we wrestle with straw monsters. We have nothing to prove because we are equal but different from the very beginning of God's plan.

A second area of distinctive difference in husbands and wives is emotional. A man and a woman will experience the same kind of emotions but express them in two different ways. You may cry; he may explode. You'll want to talk; he'll brood in silence. The reasons for this are both cultural and heredity. You may find quick release in tears, but your husband may never have felt "permission" to cry. Society does not give men this kind of permission. But your husband *does* experience emotions. Many explosive situations are aggravated when a wife doesn't give her husband permission to express himself in his own way.

At the time I wrote this book, my husband's mother was dying of cancer. Each member of the family has had their own, unique response to her suffering. Most have found expression in tears, either privately or with others. I have seen her other two sons cry, but not my husband. I have never seen him cry. But I know he grieves—either inside or privately. I can't and must not insist he "perform" in a manner acceptable to others who grieve.

Without realizing it, it *is* easy for a wife to want her

husband to become like her: sensitive, tender, caring, romantic, and communicative. All in one bundle, and NOW. Husbands *are* these things, but usually not to the extent or in the same way we are.

The husband-creature you live with is a man and, as such, will express himself in a man's unique way. We must allow him to flourish without the pressure to be something or someone he is not created to be.

Another area of difference in men and women becomes apparent in the social realm. In almost any crowd you can find men discussing social and business issues, politics, sports, and their work. These are very comfortable subjects for them. On the other hand, listen to any group of women and you will notice that they tend to discuss relationships of one form or another. Men are highly motivated by their work and working. Many women are too, yet, as a rule, women will be more relational in their interests even where work is concerned. In social settings, men don't often dwell on their families or their marriage, although women often do. This is not because men don't care, it's because they are different.

Your husband, if he's like most men, will tend to shy away from subjects dealing with "feelings." To go deeper to a level of feelings-communication is generally uncomfortable for men. I would call this a characteristic rather than a fault—an interesting facet of maleness rather than a flaw to be pointed out. Men must be carefully encouraged to communicate feelings, never threatened or mocked.

God did not make two identical creatures. Rather, He designed complementary people who would be attracted by the distinctions of the other and who would benefit from those.

25

Did God create men without the capacity to say "I love you?" No, but it seems to be difficult for some to say it out loud. They would rather express it by their caring actions or by their work. Men tend to focus on action and facts, logical deductions, and concrete ideas. *The wise wife will not demand continual verbal expressions of love,* but will take the time to observe his actions which often express hidden feelings. For some wives, action is all she will get—and it will not seem like enough. She may long for verbal or even physical affection from a husband who is *only capable* of expressing his love by faithfulness to his work and to his wife. We cannot change a man, only the power of God working in Him can make him more sensitive, more demonstrative. Since we can't change him, we must trust God's infinite grace—and work on *us.*

In the absence of verbal expressions, a wife need not despair. Remember, it is the job of God alone to meet *all* our needs. Believing this is foundational to marital happiness. When we realize and accept this, we begin to *appreciate* what our husband *does* do, and we become more thankful for all the positive qualities he *does* have. Allowing God to develop a contented spirit in you has a way of drawing out the best of loving qualities from a husband. You can help him grow not by nagging, but by praying, accepting, and assuring him of his worth. Affirmation is a golden key that can open many doors.

We've said it many times and in many ways: Men are decidedly different from women. That very diversity of the sexes is something we can learn to delight in—even to laugh at sometimes. It is, after all, what drew us to them in the first place. Men will be men. And I, for one, am glad.

Biblical Principle:
God created men to be manly and women to be
womanly. As we live out our distinctive and delightful
differences, we most fully mirror God's creative intent
(Genesis 3:16–19). "For a man...is the image and glory
of God; but the woman is the glory of man" (I Corinthians 11:7).

My Scripture:
"And God created man in His own image, in the
image of God He created him; male and female He
created them" (Genesis 1:27).

My Prayer:
"Dear Creator God, is this really true? I had no idea!
So that's why _____ is like he is! It's *you* I've
really been seeking, isn't it? I wonder what this is going
to mean to our marriage? Something tells me we've
only just begun to make *marriage* an action verb!"

SPECIAL NOTE: Flaws, shortcomings, human failures
are in a different category than physical, mental, or
emotional abuse from a husband. Under no circumstances can these actions be tolerated or excused.
Never believe *you* are the cause of these kinds of
actions. You and your children are the victims. Never
believe this kind of behavior is "normal" or that there
is no one you can tell. Begin by telling your pastor's
wife or a trusted friend, then ask for referral to counselors, agencies, church support groups, or individuals who can help. An excellent book on the topic is
*Lovestruck—Realistic Help for Battered Wives and Bruised
Homes* by Catherine Scott.

— 5 —
Women Will Be Women

Sit back and relax as we take an imaginary stroll along the green trails of the Garden of Eden. Listen to the throbbing silence of the universe at the close of day. Earth is still rosy with the blush of youth, and Eve is taking her usual walk with God. It's cool and fresh. Broad strokes of crimson brush the hairline horizon as twilight steals over the lush landscape of Eden. Leaves glisten, dark-green messengers of dusk. Plump purple lilacs perfume the garden. Eve and God finish their daily fellowship and she walks on, alone. Her happy heart settles against the loving heartbeat of God's unblemished earth. She smiles, and feels the comfortable silence in this fertile womb of all beginnings. A geyser of praise springs to her lips. Earth is a glistening jewel hung against the velvet drape of the universe. God said it is good and it is. . .*very* good.

Then came deceit, lies, sin, bruising God's world which now stands expectantly on tiptoe awaiting complete, eternal renewal. Anxious husbands and wives drive tired bodies and barter their health and happiness for "more." Now production is the new god in the garden.

In this temporary world of ours, out-of-joint and off course, God *and* beauty have taken a back seat. Technology sits on the throne.

Is there anything a woman can do to reclaim beauty in her life? Yes, I believe there is. You have a "garden" of your own which can showcase supernatural beauty and be a haven for you, your husband, and your loved ones. That garden is your home.

Never consider beauty as an "extra" your home can do without, a frivolity. Precisely *because* of our high-tech age, beauty is a necessity without which our spirits would shrivel.

Jean Lush, writing in *Focus On The Family* magazine said, "Shabbiness and disorder drain us." We all need beauty, our husbands included. We all need loveliness. And God has created woman (you!) with the unique, inborn ability to meet that need for herself and her loved ones. *You can do it!*

Beauty is a "yes" vote in a "no" world that worships at the shrine of productivity, efficiency, and busyness —a world that seldom pauses long enough to smile at a sunrise or touch a dewy leaf in awe. We all find ourselves gasping for breath in our jungle of computer terminals, billboards, neon lights, and television commercials. Seldom do we slow down long enough to appreciate beauty just because it's there.

God knows how important beauty is to the human spirit, and provides it for us in so many ways: the whiff of honeysuckle on a country lane, the friendly gurgle of a brook. We can see His handiwork in the wash of color that splashes happily over the earth at each sunrise and the parting benediction of each sunset. We can see it in the white wool of clouds, in the swaying grasses, and in the breathless music of the wind.

Our world is harmonious, beautiful, full of brilliant splendors. I watch the seasons change in my woods and see patterning, order, planning, routine, variety, and beauty.

Some of this beauty can be brought into our homes in so many ways. And most husbands will respond—even subconsciously—to such a home by wanting to be there, by enjoying the experience of being home, by going home in his mind during the work day.

Beauty is not to be equated with luxury. Very poor homes can be beautiful. Beauty does not depend on expensive furnishings or a new house. It does depend on creativity and innovation and a desire to have a beautiful home. More than any physical trappings, beauty is a feeling you get when you step into a room where things are arranged to accommodate the people living there. Beauty is cleanliness and order and harmony, with cleanliness being the basic ingredient. Just like a beautiful woman begins by caring for and cleansing her skin before she puts on makeup, a beautiful home must begin with cleanliness.

A beautiful home must not be barren. Most women have a built-in resistance to barrenness. Give us a table and we'll cover it with a pretty cloth. Give us a vase and we'll fill it with flowers. Give us a desert and we'll plant a cactus garden. It is a completely natural urge, and one some have tried to deny on our way to the market-place.

I believe this innate sense of beauty can be a wife's personal gift of love to her husband's sense of well-being. As a woman, we are somehow created to unleash blooms into our garden of life, to untie rainbows, and to splatter color and fragrance and the soft rhythm of love into our homes and our marriages.

Beauty is a link between us and God. It turns us away, for a moment, from the created to the Creator. A flower bursting into bloom shouts praises to its Maker and breeds in all of us an anticipation of heaven.

Your home can be beautiful. It can present a picture of order and harmony. It is the backdrop for a harmonious marriage and contributes subtly to it. Beauty is the song of a home. Without beauty, the song is flat, uninteresting, and even full of discord.

"The melody unfolds above the supporting column of harmony," writes Joseph Machlis about music. It's the same with a home and a marriage. The melody of a marriage must be supported by the twin columns of harmony and beauty.

A relaxed kind of order is one aspect of beauty. Disorder is inharmonious and jarring. It sets up a kind of rasping sound inside us, and, frequently, we don't know what's wrong. But it's hard to sing a song in a dump. It's hard to harmonize when you're tripping over dirty socks and shoving aside dirty dishes to get to the clean ones.

Constant and unchanging clutter is an enemy of harmony and a key factor in unhappy marriages. Clutter is distracting, confusing, discordant; it clashes with something inside us. Where clutter is constant, the melody of a marriage can become forced, choked. When the man in your life *never* knows what he will be stepping on when he walks through the door, something needs to change. At least a semblance of order is vital to his sense of well-being—and yours, too!

One lovely, talented, and vivacious wife brought a new twinkle of husbandly joy to her husband's eye simply by deciding to have a clean white shirt ready for each of his work days ahead of time—to eliminate the daily hassle. It made him feel like a king...and want to treat her like a queen. Your circumstances may be different, yet there are few places where the principle of creating beauty cannot be applied.

Whether you do these things yourself or hire them done is not the point either. Seeing to it that it happens is the point. Seeing to it that your "nest" is a place you both want to come home to is a worthy goal.

If creating beauty does not come naturally to you, find a friend and ask her advice. Look for someone who has created a "user-friendly," pleasant home and ask her advice. Ask her to walk through your house and give you ideas for beautifiying it. Or, if your budget allows, hire a decorator. You might also go to the home of someone you know is a natural organizer and watch her work some day; ask her questions; or hire her to teach you to organize. Maybe you could trade a skill or service for help.

If home care is your responsibility, but you find organization a *big* problem, turn to others who have conquered this problem. Pam Young and Peggy Jones are two ladies who present mini-workshops for churches, clubs, and conventions. They also have a bi-monthly newsletter, *She's On Track.* (Write to P.O. Box 5364, Vancouver, WA 98668, or call (206) 696-4091.) Their book is entitled *Sidetracked Home Executives* (Warner Books).

Beauty shows in small ways: a vase of fresh flowers (or even pretty weeds), colors that make you happy, music playing quietly, a candlelight dinner with the phone unplugged, the television off, and the kids in bed. These things breed peace, contentment, and a sense of place. Both partners feel they "belong" here. It's a place where needs are met.

Music provides a beautiful atmosphere (depending on the kind, of course). Without even realizing it, our spirits can be nourished by music. Meals go better against a background of instrumental music. Music soothes, restores, and even inspires worship. Music encourages romance. It administers a kind of grace in mysterious ways and lights a candle in our souls.

Laughter is also beauty. What soothing relief comes in a good laugh! What joy! Laughter takes the sharp edge off sorrow and failure; it helps us not to take ourselves too seriously. Proverbs 17:22 tells us a "joyful heart is good medicine." Learn to laugh with your mate and you will have discovered a precious secret to creating a beautiful atmosphere.

In the back of my head I hear the clamor: Busy, too busy, my life is just too busy! I know it is. Is there anything you can do about it? Yes. It's a matter of choice. This man you married should get first place in your attentions. What's preventing it? Is it *that* important? Does it have to be forever?

Look for ways to make your home beautiful, both in decor and in atmosphere. Let your home reach out and smile at the occupants. May it say, "Hello, I've been waiting for you. Come on in. This is our sanctuary. Let's enjoy it togther."

Biblical Principle:
Orderliness and beauty contribute to contentment.

My Scripture:
"But let all things be done properly and in an orderly manner" (I Corinthians 14:40).

My Prayer:
"Here I sit, Lord, wondering where to start. I'm busy, Lord. Maybe too busy. Maybe too busy because I'm

unorganized. Slow me down, Father. Show me how to grow roses out of these ashes and to stop long enough to smell their fragrance."

— 6 —
Becoming A Woman Of Beauty

Any strong chain is made up of lots of individual links. Any strong marriage is made up of lots of different pieces. Each one is absolutely necessary to the overall strength of the chain—or marriage. Looking feminine, like the woman you are, is one of those links in a strong marriage. God created men and women to be attractive to one another, and there is everything right about a balanced approach to making yourself attractive.

The Beauty of Clothing

"She makes coverings for herself; her clothing is fine linen and purple" (Proverbs 31:22).

One husband told me, "My wife makes a concerted effort to be attractive. She's neat and clean and sweet-smelling, which to me, spells attractive. I know she does this for herself *and* for me, but what it does for me is boost my morale. Somehow, when I see her standing there all feminine and pretty and smelling *so* nice, it assures me *my* world is together. I have to work in old clothes, and I get into a lot of just plain dirty work, but it does something very special to me to see her like that. It makes me feel like a man, and I don't even know why."

Did your ears perk up when you read that last sentence? Go ahead, read it again. This man's statement explains a husband's response to his wife in the physical realm of attraction. It *does* matter how you present yourself to him.

There was a late 1989 ad that said, "Want him to be more of a man? Try being more of a woman." Frankly, there's a lot of truth in that terse statement.

The same man who made the previous comments said, "My wife sets the tone for our home even by the way she dresses. She doesn't have expensive clothes or dress in a flashy manner, but she's clean, reasonably stylish, attractive, and modest. We [the family] look to her, in a sense, for guidance and a kind of inspiration. She's our pacesetter."

It really does seem that women are innately able to add softness and flair to almost anything they wear, whether it's a scarf, a pin, or a brocade vest. Even tailored clothing, completed by a feminine touch can become pure poetry. The extra effort does affect both you and your husband. A woman's clothing is the whisper of her inner spirit.

When dressing, be as natural as sunlight, as fragrant as air, as lyrical as a melody drifting over a secluded lake at dusk. Be clean and classic. Be playfully lovely to look at. Be modest and mysterious. Be starched and white, elegant and fresh, sassy and succulent. At different times, different places, indulge a mood in your dressing. Add a flower here, a bit of lace there, a brooch on a belt, any little bit of fanfare that says you are a woman.

One Sunday while dressing for church, I realized I had no jewelry to match my daisy yellow skirt and wildflower blouse. I reached for a yellow scarf, twisted it, and tied it around my neck in a knot. Then, I pulled two lavender morning glories from an arrangement on my dresser and attached them to the yellow scarf with a pearl hatpin through the center of each lavender flower. It was a perfect color match, and I felt wonderful and complete.

Part of the lyrical mystery of being a woman *can* be expressed in our dress. . .as a study of one of the most romantic books of poetry can tell you—*The Song of Solomon*. Every once in awhile, take your husband's breath away absolutely on purpose! Create a circle of magic that's only big enough for two. Sweep him off his feet entirely—your way. There's no reason YOU shouldn't be the "girl of his dreams."

Modesty, for the Christian wife, should also be a primary consideration. It's important to dress in such a way that you feel confident and able to *forget* yourself once you leave the mirror. Women have revealed so much for so long that it is no longer seductive *or* attractive. Now, modesty is the shocker rather than immodesty. A woman who dresses in such a way that she is both beautiful and modest is a woman with *true* feminine allure. Her husband will be drawn to her and be proud of her. And, he will not be afraid for her to be around other men because he knows she is not dressing in a way that will distract them or lead them into unsavory thoughts. The way we dress should *adorn* Christ and draw attention to the positive difference He makes in our lives. Remember the key to true beauty as a child of God—"the king's daughter is all glorious *within*" (Psalm 45:13).

The Beauty of Fragrance

Scent is love in a crystal flacon: A fragrant expression of womanly artistry and a subtle reminder of romance.

"To me," said Robert Ricci, perfume baron, "perfume is an art form, like music which stirs our souls, pulls our heartstrings, brings memories to our minds." Psalm 45:8 says, "All thy garments are fragrant with myrrh and aloes and cassia." The Song of Solomon 1:12 says, "While the king was at his table, my perfume gave forth its fragrance;" 4:17 says, "Your lips, my bride, drip honey. . .and the fragrance of your garments is like the fragrance of Lebanon."

Envelop yourself in earth's own sweet perfumes: floral, woodsy, musk, or spice. All come from the bouquet of Earth and are given to us to enhance our lives and that of those we love.

You might keep a pretty container of scented potpourri near your bedside or on your desk. Simmer a little on your stove. Surround yourself in fragrance that inspires you *and* your mate. Try the light florals on hot days, and deeper, more lingering fragrances for winter. Switch to the bright change of spice as your mood dictates. Be sure to wear your husband's favorite at bedtime and other special times whenever possible. Fragrances are a link in your chain of love.

Among my memorabilia is a beautifully boxed flacon of perfume given to me over twenty-eight years ago by my, then, fiance. When I open the container, the fragrance begins an instant memory journey for me back to where our love began.

Remember the scent you wore when you dated your husband? It will always belong to the both of you, won't it? Get a bottle of it if you can and save it for very special occasions: anniversaries, the birth of a child, loving moments. Wearing it every day would dilute its impact, but it can be to your husband like a fresh-picked bouquet of romantic notions.

The Beauty of a Quiet Place

If you are like most of us, you need a quiet place to call your own occasionally. And, like most of us, you probably re-create best in quietness. But most of us, even though we need solitude, resist it. We're afraid, I think, of whom we will see there and what we will learn.

If solitude is a stranger to you, take it a bit at a time until it's comfortable. A few minutes now. A few hours later on. Relax into the stillness of a moment completely. Fall into a vortex of quietness, the pillow of timelessness. Breathe deeply, again and again, and close your eyes to the world outside. Come away. . . .

Now and then, we need to lean back into the bosom of God and His creation and let the dew of creative quietness restore us. The Bible encourages it. "He leads me beside quiet waters. He restores my soul. . ." (Psalm 23:2–3). The Lord Jesus went to a lonely place to pray, to talk to the Father (Mark 1:35). It is in solitude that we can nurture "the hidden person of the heart, with the imperishable quality of a gentle and quiet spirit, which is precious in the sight of God" (I Peter 3:4).

Where could a quiet place for you be? A walkway? A bathtub? The feminine ritual is soothing to the body in its warm, silky, serene solitude. Or, it could be the tranquility of a private space, maybe a library nook or a beach on a cloudy day. A garden or a country park. A drive in the country. Perhaps a park bench and a brown bag lunch at noon.

Author Merle Shain shares her thoughts on the subject in *Courage My Love*. "There isn't a paradise someone can lead us to unless it's the world we make for ourselves." Her spots of tranquility include a room on her top floor, "curtained with vines and garlanded with lace."

My own favorite spots include a homemade rocking chair on our wide front porch, or the swing on our summer porch (especially during a gentle rain). Then there's my office loft which, like Merle Shain's room, is "curtained with vines." Here I sit, high as the treetops, watching the squirrels play and the birds romance each other while looking for nesting material.

Do you have a place to "nest"? Can you find one?

Take a substantial pleasure in becoming the woman your husband loves to linger near. It's just *one* of the pleasures of being a woman.

Biblical Principle:

A godly woman respects her body as the temple of God, respects herself as a child of the King, and respects her husband by her grooming.

My Scripture:

"Do you not know that your body is a temple of the Holy Spirit who is in you, whom you have from God, and that you are not your own? For you have been bought with a price: therefore glorify God in your body" (I Corinthians 6:19-20).

My Prayer:

"Dear Father, help me take a good look at myself. . . in every area. Show me where I can make changes and where I have to accept things I can't change. Make me over, Lord, so that you shine out through the very best of me."

— 7 —
Permission To Be A Woman

"The *right* kinds of manliness and womanliness are
something to hold on to."
Elizabeth Cody Newenhuyse
"A Kiss and 7-Up"
Marriage Partnership, Spring 1988

I picked the magazine off the drugstore shelf, intrigued by the beautiful glossy cover and the title:
"Victoria." It was nostalgic, genteel somehow. Something about it pulled at me, but I didn't know what it
was. In a private moment I opened it and browsed
through page after page of exquisite scenery, mood
pictures, still life paintings, and even floral scented
pages. When I was through, I leaned back refreshed,
and wondered why I felt so serene—unhurried.

I thought about the other magazines on my book-
shelf. Many of them informed me and educated me.
Others entertained me or took me shopping in the
fashion world, making me want everything I saw.
Some gave me ways to cram more into my days and
then ways to relieve the stress caused by doing just that.

Some had fattening recipes and aerobic exercise tips in the same issue. Each gave me ways to be a better me, as if the "me" I was didn't quite make it. What was it about this new magazine?

Then, suddenly, I knew. This magazine gave me permission to be a woman! Unique in the annals of American magazines, it had touched a chord long untouched and said, "It's okay to thrill to the touch of lace." It said, "It's perfectly all right to dream in the moonlight." It told me, "Go ahead and be dazzled by a field of wildflowers. Relax; it's fine to feel womanly and tender when you see a baby and to be struck speechless at the beauty of a white swan on a pond." It even gave me permission to curl up in an easy chair (in a white frock!), sip lemonade, and read a good book! Hooray!

I recklessly subscribed, along with thousands of others grown tired of too many years of "dress for success." The response of women all over the country was astonishing. And the message was clear: We are ready, once again, to be fully woman.

Had the pressure of women's rights made us all feel overwhelmed by a loss of identity—a kind of worthlessness, even guilt, about our womanhood? Had it directed us and encouraged us to envy everything about a man and deny it was any fun to be a woman?

I don't know about you, but I'm afraid something happened to me on the way to the office—something slow, like the dripping of a faucet that you don't really hear until the house is completely quiet. Our world is quieter now, and we can all hear the drip. Now we know where the flood came from and why we feel the way we do. We're wondering where our womanliness "got to." And, I'm afraid, so are our husbands. Somehow, we know it's time to reclaim it.

Womanliness Defined

What do I mean by womanliness? I mean that ineffable, soft quality of being a woman with a *woman's* heart. I mean being feminine, acting like it, and enjoying it. Femininity—womanliness—is enchanting! It is a pearl of great price, and built right inside us by God himself.

To put it in other ways, womanliness is:

- A rose not masquerading as a cornstalk.
- A peacock not going underground as a worm.
- A tender touch not disguised in boxing gloves.
- Grace in glass slippers instead of wingtips.
- Satin and silk as often as denim.

Mull these words over as you draw a picture of a woman: Elegance, graciousness, symmetry, refinement, charm, playfulness, style, comeliness, radiance, loveliness, tenderness, compassion, sensitivity, enchantment, taste, purity, culture, emotional, attractiveness, vivaciousness, hospitality, gentleness, kindness, restraint, winsomeness, grace, cordiality. Womanliness is all these traits and more. A certain degree of each one of these qualities came with your birth certificate. How much they have flowered is another thing.

Womanliness is the basket of flowers beside the peanut butter sandwich. It's the music in the windstorm. It's the powder on the puff, the cream in the coffee, the icing on the cake. It's the waltz instead of the march, the lace on the glove, the harp and not the hammer. It's the extra-special-something in you that makes a husband's world go 'round a lot more happily.

Womanliness goes so much deeper than makeup or clothes. It begins in the inner chambers of your soul where the footprints of God are. As your fellowship with Him intensifies, the beauty of your godly, womanly character blossoms, letting your feminine qualities be cut and polished like the precious jewels God created them to be. Indeed, the real *you* shines, not your clothes, no matter how spectacular they are. It is *you* who adorns your clothing. Your innate character, your winsome womanliness will be the deciding factor in whether you *truly* "look good."

The psalmist wrote, "The King's daughter is all glorious within" (45:13). Inspired by God, King Solomon wrote eloquently of his bride. Womanhood is our "garment," our cloak, our coat of many colors.

Consider the "cloak" of the woman in so many television programs. She is the dominant force in the relationship (which is usually not marriage). She is selfish, demanding, full of cute quips and sassy back-talk. She is sensual—but she is not womanly. She contributes to society's continual blurring of roles and a distortion of authentic love between husbands and wives. She is obsessed with immediate physical gratification, and, if the scripting is to be believed, it dominates her entire life. She is a creation of the media to some extent, but unfortunately, she also reflects the lifestyle of many. She is not a godly woman. She does not model womanliness.

I am glad to know there *is* a choice. We don't have to be like these television women in order to be "current." God created woman with a fuller, broader purpose than just being sensual or propagating the human race. He made us to be treasured, adored, respected. He wants us (and our husbands) to delight in the garden of us—our womanhood—with all its inherent privileges. He wants us to reclaim the lost territory which right-fully belongs to those God created female.

Perhaps as you read *Irresistible Wifestyles*, you may sense a new voice calling you to be fully feminine again. . .without apology. If so, LISTEN. Listen deeply and well. It may be your womanhood calling.

Biblical Principle:
    Woman was created to fill, or complete, the need in man and can only do that well as she becomes fully woman in the image God designed for her.

My Scripture:
    "Like an apple tree among the trees of the forest, so is my beloved among the young men. . . .He has brought me to his banquet hall, and his banner over me is love" (Song of Solomon 2:3–4).

My Prayer:
    "What a relief, Lord! I didn't even realize how much I was denying my womanly instincts or why. It's almost like I can feel something special bubbling up inside me, trying to spill over. . .and I like the feeling. Will you unlock my woman's nature all the way, and help me be the kind of woman my husband will adore? Thank you."

— 8 —
Womanliness Reclaimed

Where does this chapter find you? Can you relax into your femininity and find joy in being a woman? Can you walk past the role models created by the media and dare to be a woman after *God's* own heart? Can you reclaim yourself and your gender out of an age when male/female roles are blurred and confusing? And if you can, and after you accept it in your heart, will you act it out in your marriage?

Sit back and get ready for a ride you may not have taken in a while. This short chapter will be a clarion call to reclaim your womanhood as God created it for you. It will be a call to role definition and expression. It will challenge you to exert the full power—and privileges—of your womanliness.

Are you, even in the least, intrigued? Well then, come along. Let's have some heart-to-heart "girl talk."

As we've already established, God created men to need *women*. Look at your own husband. He married a woman. He married everything you are as a woman. Everything you were given naturally by God exerted a pull in him toward you. It's awesomely God-given.

Now, think back. When your husband indicated that he wanted to spend his life with you, was it because he needed a housekeeper? Do you think it was because he needed a caretaker for his future (or present) children? I think it's safe to say he married you out of a far deeper need than either of these things. He also married you out of a far deeper urge than mere physical attraction, although I think we may safely assume that was also there. He saw in you (whether or not he could articulate it) a kind of female answer to his male questions. He sensed in you, a woman, someone who was the other half of his manhood. Your feminine nature was the ultimate, final attraction. He responded to you out of his God-designed need for your womanliness.

The Creation account in Genesis 1 and 2 is plain about *why* God created womankind. Man *needed* her. God created the kind of creature who had all the particular qualities Adam (and all men after him) would need. Characteristics and abilities He didn't give them. If woman became anything less than she was created to be, both the man and the woman would suffer loss. And we see that today. Womanhood *has* suffered tremendous losses, and so have our marriages.

I look around me and see distorted, teetering marriages where the husband doesn't *think* he needs a wife. Too many seem to think they need more income and see her as a source of supply, then insist that she fill that role.

I see homes in pain because the wife has not recognized *her need* of her husband's maleness, and where she has run roughshod over him, becoming the self-appointed decision-maker. Not encouraging him to be the head of the marriage (Ephesians 5:23).

Thankfully, we still see some beautiful examples of happy, long-term marriages where each partner realizes and enjoys his or her unique creative role, acknowledging a *need* for the other. Making the most of their God-given partnership.

I look back to Genesis chapters one and two and see in this creative plan of God a grand, sweeping, open-armed permission to be a woman: to talk like one, walk like one, cry like one, dress like one, and live like one.

As part of Satan's evil corruption of the human race, this permission has been denied in today's increasingly sexless culture. Instead, society at large urges us to be aggressive, defiant, dominant, selfish, unfaithful. We've been given the green light to devalue virginity and even to be ashamed of it. We've been encouraged to be consumed by a loveless lust and to believe somehow that one man and one woman plus the act of copulation equals love. It is a sweeping and masterful deception by Satan that has produced fragmentation of the family, pain, and disruption to the plan of God for our marriages.

Our sensitive, womanly natures have been tossed back and forth in the winds of change. They have been assaulted and bruised long enough. Haven't you felt the woman nature in you cry out to God, somehow knowing His plan is best after all?

Let's consider the question once again: Am I ready to relax into my God-given femininity and let God direct my life as He originally intended? Think about it a few minutes. Are you ready to tough it out with His blueprint for womanhood and let your private world begin a turnaround? Are you ready to rejoice in your femininity, your purity, faithfulness, commitment, integrity of womanhood, love, and respect? As "revolutionary" as these may seem, they are on the cutting edge of Christianity today. They are daring watchwords that will set you apart and label you.

It is when we put this vocabulary to work in any life that we have the golden keys to a winsome wifery that works.

Is it any wonder that each key has been snatched away or twisted, one by one, by the father of lies? It's his job, after all, to destroy marriages, especially those joined by God. And Satan's vocabulary has gotten a lot of free press: lust, cheating, "love" affair, contractual marriage, Me first, freedom of choice.

I, for one, am outraged at Satan's tactics and done with the crude, lustful "love" of television which distorts real love and destroys respect between the sexes.

Does this arouse your indignation? Are you ready, even a little bit, to reclaim your womanliness and to live it out as fully as you can? Are you prepared to enjoy yourself and your natural role more completely?

If this is a new emphasis in your life, and if, by God's grace, you begin to blossom as a woman, watch out! This is a radical message. But God has always chosen to work at marriage from the inside out rather than the outside in. He's the one who invented our roles and marriage. He's the only authentic expert on the subject.

On the road to enhanced personal womanliness, don't be surprised if life within your four walls becomes even more interesting. And don't be surprised if, on the way, you and your husband find some altogether new shades of the rainbow you may not have seen for some time.

Don't squash your femininity. Don't be ashamed to be a woman. Don't cover it as you would a scar. Let it blossom in ways of your own choosing, ways that become *you*, and become a sweet fragrance to all who see your marriage in renewal.

Biblical Principle:

God created women to be women. A wife who is creatively feminine will be a marriage builder.

My Scripture:

"An excellent wife, who can find? For her worth is far above jewels. The heart of her husband trusts in her, and he will have no lack of gain" (Proverbs 31:10–11).

My Prayer:

"I think I'm getting the picture, Lord. I think I've been wrong. I thought that if I really let go and enjoyed my womanhood, I would be trampled on and considered inferior. I thought I had to imitate men in order to "make it." I've been working so hard at trying to bury my feminine responses—as though they were inferior instead of just different. It sort of scares me, though. Still. . .I hear a faint wind blowing. . .and there's a song in the wind just for me. Teach me how to be your woman, all the way. . . .Teach me, because I think I have a lot to learn."

Part 2

Christ is the Cornerstone—knowing Him intimately is the key.

— 9 —
Beginning With Christ

Coming to Christ for forgiveness and receiving it is a spiritual and wonder-filled experience. Who among us can really comprehend what God Almighty performs in our souls when we invite Him to be Lord of all?

To invite Christ into our lives as Savior and to become an heir of eternal life and a child of the Creator is a fearful and glorious thing. Who can *really* understand?

If you have already come to this magnificent Lord, read the following as a reminder and rejoice in the touchstone of your faith.

If you have not met this Jesus in a personal way, He comes to you with open arms of forgiveness and an insistent love that refuses to die—a love that drew blood and squeezed life from Him.

Wherever this finds you, read on, and know the Christ who meets you where you are, with unquenchable, unconditional love.

A Parable Of You and Me
"Whoever drinks of the water that I shall give him shall never thirst; but the water that I shall give him shall become in him a well of water springing up to eternal life."

Jesus. . .can you see Him standing, arms extended, a gentle breeze ruffling his garments? His eyes bathe you in love, and in His right hand is a pitcher overflowing with living water. It's a silvery, musical waterfall, and it never ends. The source of the flow comes from within the Master Himself (John 4:14). Unbearable thirst drives you forward as He offers the water to you. You move forward, throat parched and eyes fastened on the pitcher. You want to offer Him something. Your time? He's not interested. Your energy then? He shakes His head. You reach into your purse. Your money, surely? He shakes His head again and extends the water. You look into His eyes, and then you know. It is free, this water, and you are humbled into an impotent silence.

Is there nothing at all you can give for the water then? His words echo in your mind: "For God so loved the world that He gave His only begotten Son, that whoever believes in Him should not perish, but have eternal life" (John 3:16).

Other words like the rushing of a mighty wind tumble from His lips. "Blessed are those who hunger and thirst for righteousness, for they shall be satisfied" (Matthew 5:6). "I am the door; if anyone enters through Me, he shall be saved, and shall go in and out, and find pasture" (John 10:9). "If any man is thirsty, let him come to Me and drink" (John 7:37).

The words hurt, yet stir a strange longing. You were so sure you had so much to give in exchange for this water. You move closer and fall to your knees, suddenly the supplicant, admitting your total need of this Jesus and the water of life that flows from Him. You have tried to fill yourself with living water: a little church attendance here, a little Bible reading there, good works when possible or convenient. But now it's different. Now you have come to *Him*. Before you merely tasted at the tributaries and bypassed the headwaters. Suddenly, completely, convicted of your pretense and pride, you know it is Christ and Him alone you need.

"Come to Me, all who are weary and heavy laden, and I will give you rest" (Matthew 11:28). The words, felt as much as spoken, penetrate your heart and echo again and again until you begin to understand. Christ Himself, the Cornerstone, is your source of true life. He is your beginning and your end. To move through life without Him is to be thirsty and parched and dry and brittle and shriveled. And so you have been.

Tears flow as you open yourself fully to the Master. Then comes the living water. You think you will drown in the abundance of it. You don't know how long you kneel there, silent, awed, then finally at peace.

The water fills you, and the Master is smiling. You feel His smile surging through you in a strange, new way. Then, you can contain no more! Your cup overflows. You look, and streams of living water have begun to flow out from you—and yet you are not diminished, because they flow without end into you from Jesus.

You rise and walk away, feeling very strong. The water within you continues to flow out to others in silvery tributaries. You laugh with the pure joy of it all. Then, you notice something. These thirsty people are only drinking from your tributaries. And they can never seem to get enough. You shout, pointing to the Master who is in plain view. You try to tell them He has water that will completely quench their thirst, but they won't listen, just as you hadn't. It's true you have a drink to give them, but it won't last. Not like His. They will only get thirsty again. "Master!" You shout again. "Tell them!"

55

"I have," He says softly.

You turn around for a last look at the Savior, and still He waits. A few have come. Multitudes have not. They don't seem to see Him, or if they do, they pass on by.

Then, in alarm, you look at your own stream. It has shrunken to a trickle. You are only a short journey from the Master, and yet it trickles. Then you know you must stay closer to Him—must return again and again to the mainstream that flows from and is Christ if your stream is to flow full and free.

"Jesus!" You speak His name in an urgent whisper and point to your stream. Suddenly you are again immersed in His power. He is the giver. You are the receiver. You feel the power in increasing measure as you stay at His feet and allow the water of His own Holy Spirit to work in you. He speaks a last time before you descend the mountain.

"You shall know that I am in My Father, and you in Me, and I in you. . . .But the Helper, the Holy Spirit, whom the Father will send in My name, He will teach you all things, and bring to your remembrance all that I said to you. Peace I leave with you. My peace I give to you; not as the world gives, do I give to you. Let not your heart be troubled, nor let it be fearful" (John 14:20,26–27).

Biblical Principle:

Christ alone gives salvation and provides power to live the Christian life victoriously.

My Scripture:

"If any man is thirsty, let him come to Me and drink. He who believes in Me, as the Scripture said, 'From his

innermost being shall flow rivers of living water' "
(John 7:37–38).

My Prayer:
"My Jesus, I love you. I *know* I am yours. . .but, oh,
Lord, I haven't obeyed you the way I should have and
I'm starving for renewed fellowship. You know, the
kind we used to have. I've wandered away—and it feels
so far. Lord Jesus, take your rightful throne in my life.
Be King of my life again so that others can see you
flowing in and out of me."

If You Are Coming To Christ:
"Lord God, I have not seen you this way before! I
ache with my sin, but I feel the power of your love.
Forgive me, Lord Jesus. I believe in you, in who you
are. I give myself wholly and fully to you. You died for
me. Rose again from the dead. Incredible, wonder-
filled truths! Forgive me, Lord Jesus. Invade my life.
I'm yours."

— 10 —
Going Deeper

We begin with Christ. . .but then there's the rest of the journey. And a great part of that journey takes place as we relate to our husbands. The setting is the home—our space—our territory. How are things at your home? I mean really? How is the harmony factor?

It's true that no home will ever be heaven as long as we live on earth, but most homes can be *more* heavenly than they are. As wives, we can have a lot to do with it. In fact, the power we have as just one person in the home is both exciting and very scary. God gives us His orders in Scripture that go like this: "Live in harmony with one another" (Romans 12:16, NIV). "If it is possible, as far as it depends on you, live at peace with everyone" (Romans 12:18, NIV). Because these orders come from God Himself, we can be sure He gives power to accomplish that which He has commanded.

I think about Snow White when I think of harmony. Remember her fanciful little cottage where she and all her animal friends sang and whistled their way through the dusting and vacuuming? She and those seven little dwarfs plus the menagerie of animals lived *so harmoniously.* But she was a fairy tale, and we are not; so we're left to find some practical means to create harmony and peace in our homes.

Would you classify yourself as a peacemaker? If you're like most of us, at times you are, and sometimes you're not. But do you *aim* for harmony or discord? "Peacemakers who sow in peace raise a harvest of righteousness" (James 3:18, NIV). How's your harvest?

"His divine power has given us everything we need for life and godliness through our knowledge of him who called us by his own glory and goodness" (II Peter 1:3). But what is godliness anyway, when the "rubber meets the road?"

Some I know would answer that question by listing the things they do or don't do. They would recite the places they don't visit and activities they don't attend. They would point to the number of Bibles on their shelves and the regularity of their church attendance. But these things are only externals. They don't necessarily say a thing about the state of the heart. God's eyesight pierces through externals like these to the very vortex of our being and asks, "Why?" He goes straight to the motive of our actions because that's where godliness begins.

Proverbs 31 paints a picture of a vigorous woman who does an awful lot of right things. Look at her impressive list of accomplishments. She selects, works, brings, provides, earns, buys, trades, gives, sews, makes, sells. But it is not her *activities* which label her forever as "a woman who fears the Lord" (verse 30). Rather, she *does* the activities because she already is a godly woman.

We are not godly because of what we do or what we don't do. Godliness is much deeper than outward actions. It is a matter of the heart, produced by a close walk with the Lord Jesus Christ. Godliness begins in private, where all the significant transactions between God and His children occur.

Think with me as we mull these things over. God is the source of godliness. Church is the source of fellowship and learning. Jobs are the source of busyness (and so are families!). Music is a source of blessedness. Rules are the source of orderliness perhaps, but not the source of holiness. Rules make you uniform—not necessarily unified. Rules make you like all the others who keep the same list. God-likeness is another matter. Only God can make us godly.

Writing in *Secret Of A Happy Christian's Life*, Hannah Whitehall Smith says, "Our main work is surrender." And the surrender she speaks of is not a once-for-all experience but a day-by-day necessity. Each morning we have the chance to surrender or to choose our own way. Throughout the day we have the opportunity to obey our Lord or to follow our own paths.

"Abide in *Me*", says Jesus, "and I will abide in you" (John 15:4). Each time we surrender our will to God's will, our way to His way, we deepen the habit of surrender and our lives look more and more like Jesus'. This, then, is where godly wives begin their journey to harmony and peace in the home.

Surrender. Submission. It hurts both our pride and our knees. But kneeling before God's throne is where surrender begins and where power begins at the same time. Presenting our hearts is much more fearsome and risky than just attending church each Sunday— and so much more exciting and full of potential. Have you ever wondered what God might really do with just one fully surrendered Christian wife?

Harmony, in essence, flows through our lives from the presence of the Holy Spirit in our hearts. The song begins there, a weak note at first perhaps, but swelling into a symphony of matchless sound as we write music into the lives of others. . .especially those in our homes.

Hard? Without question. You get no badges for this kind of private heart work. No one really knows—at least at first. But as the harmony of your life flows into your husband's life and your home, you one day find yourself allied to an entire orchestra of lives, each playing the same song but in different parts. *That's* harmony!

You won't be uniform, but you will be unified. You won't be exactly alike, but you will be blended in values and purpose. You won't be perfect, but you will be on the right road—improving with practice and sounding better all the time.

As Christian wives, we must go to the cross in prayer frequently. There, we can let go of our plans, our desires, our wills. As we lay each item down, we let go of our expectations and schemes and demands. When we can pray, "*Your* will be done, on earth, as it is in heaven," and then *let go*, we surrender our sin and our self. We acknowledge our dependency on Him. It is then that we can feel His arms around us. It is then that we claim His forgiveness and begin to live as one forgiven would live: cleansed and free. Then He begins to tie up the loose ends in our life and produce a balanced, godly life others may notice before we do.

Our Lord won't houseclean in a dusty, cobwebby life without permission, but when He does, it will be thorough!

Biblical Principle:
Walking closely with Christ produces inner peace which helps create harmonious homes.

My Scripture:
"There is. . .joy for those who promote peace" (Proverbs 12:20, NIV).

My Prayer:
"Take me down, Lord, deeper and deeper into the melodious recesses of yourself. As much as I know how, I surrender myself to you in every area of my life, and wait for your work in my life and my marriage."

— 11 —
Speak The Truth

If there is a time for everything, and God's Word says there is (Ecclesiastes 3:1), then there is also a time within a marriage to speak out clearly and in love. There are times to adapt and times to laugh; times to sing and times to love. There are also times to "level" with your partner. Not to level would be wrong. . .a lie. No matter what else we may try to call it.

The very balance of life and Scripture calls strongly and purely for lives of honesty and forthrightness. Open, clean talk. Unfuzzy words. No double meanings. No hidden agendas. No private wishes. No subtle coloring and shading of words hoping the meaning will be "caught," so it won't need to be spoken out loud.

Plain truth stands tall. It is unvarnished, clear, transparent and honest. This kind of truth isn't a bundle of words we are *supposed* to say, such as, "The kids are fine, praise the Lord." It's what we *really* feel and experience and want and should say because it is truth, even when it is words like, "Karen needs you badly."

Truth-telling may reveal us as someone with rough edges or a lack of maturity, or a shortage of understanding or incorrect doctrine. But it at least reveals and doesn't cover up. We become more transparent and vulnerable. We give ourselves permission to grow.

Truth is *real* talk that works.

"To be honest, honey, I *hate* that color."

"I feel angry because you didn't call me."

"I don't want another child just yet."

Talking truth is risky. No doubt about it. Speaking truth to a husband uncovers the real wife—the one under the lipstick and designer clothes. It may open a wife to criticism or misunderstanding. But truth clears the air. There is no mystery. Truth erases unanswered questions. Answers doubts. Relieves fear. Truth gives a couple somewhere to start. Remember I Corinthians 13:6? "Love does not delight in evil but rejoices with the truth."

When a wife offers a half-truth to her husband, she deceives herself, her mate, and God. She quenches the work of the Holy Spirit, the Spirit of truth who wants to guide us into all truth (John 16:13). She puts her spiritual life on hold.

Consider the difference.

"Oh, I guess it doesn't matter where we go."

Or, "I know you like this place, but to be honest, I'd prefer to go _____."

Maybe she *shouldn't* mind, but she does mind, and she has spoken gently, plainly so no rage is seething below ground. There is no way to misunderstand what she means. A husband can't proceed and then be shocked at his wife's beastly attitude later.

Satan, the father of lies, is the initiator and inventor of the passive half-truth so common in Christian relationships. The truth of it is that half-truths are whole lies. God calls it sin.

The naturally passive wife finds it relatively easy to obey the command in Ephesians 5:22 to submit to her husband. She finds it extremely difficult to "speak the truth in love" (Ephesians 4:15) when it means confronting her real feelings as well as her husband. In fact, we wives much prefer to shove our feelings and desires underground, believing *this* is submission and is right. But then we discover that ignoring them doesn't make them go away. They always return in different disguises because they haven't been expressed or dealt with. They come back with new names, too: resentment, an unforgiving spirit, jealousy, bitterness, rage. We may find ourselves dealing with these emotions over and over rather than looking below the surface at the root of the sin. We may find ourselves continually hacking at the weeds and never pulling out the roots.

Consider: "Go ahead, take the trip with the boys. No problem." A lie. Enter: anger, hostility, blame, frigidity, self-pity.

Consider: "I don't think it would be good for you to go at this time because. . . ."

A husband deserves truth whether he understands it or not. Even whether he believes it or not.

Consider: "John always takes his wife out to a motel during their anniversary week. Isn't that nice?" Cloaked innuendo.

"Could we go to a motel for our anniversary this year? I really would like that."

Clear question. Plain truth.

Jesus Christ said, "I am the way and the truth, and the life," (John 14:6). Truth-telling is a sign we are growing up, becoming more Christ-like (Ephesians 4:15). Cunning, craftiness, deceit, and scheming have no place in the wife-life of a believer. Truthing does.

"Rather, we have renounced secret and shameful ways; we do not use deception, nor do we distort the

65

word of God. On the contrary, by setting forth the truth plainly we commend ourselves to every man's conscience in the sight of God" (II Corinthians 4:2, NIV). By the grace of God, truth can be spoken in love and humility, with gentleness. *But it must be spoken.*

Truth is a cleansing agent, purifying relationships. A wife who *expresses,* not *represses* truth, keeps the garbage from piling up around the foundations of her marriage. In an open relationship where partners tell the truth with a loving spirit, God's Spirit can move clearly.

Submission, to many Christian wives, is a cave where they can cloak feelings they wish weren't there. Cowardice and a lying spirit can masquerade as submission. Misunderstood submission can be a rug under which we sweep truths that need to be spoken. Improperly understood submission can become a Christian catch-all to hide us from ourselves and our mates because we can't face the truth of who we are, and we don't want him to find out either. A silent submission may *act* like all is well, but the silent lie covers a thousand lies, pushed down and snap-capped.

Submission, misunderstood, has been used by many wives as an emotional closet in which to hide, a place of self-pity. But our God did not author this kind of submission which never speaks its mind because it is afraid. He is balance. He is wisdom. He tells us to let our "yes" be "yes" and our "no" be "no." "For God did not give us a spirit of timidity, but a spirit of power, of love and of self-discipline" (II Timothy 1:7, NIV).

A wife who is eager to enjoy her marriage fully and to experience life at its richest will do her part by speaking the truth in love to her mate as well as to others. She will step confidently out of her hiding places and believe that her opinions and ideas and wishes are important. She will also believe that where there is an irreconcilable difference of opinion and a decision must be made, she should defer to the final authority of her husband who himself must bear the consequences of his decision before the Lord. And the wise, loving wife will never say, "I told you so."

Biblical Principle:
Christian wives have a responsibility before God and their husbands to live honestly.

My Scripture:
"And in him you too are being built together to become a dwelling in which God lives by his Spirit" (Ephesians 2:22).

My Prayer:
"I've been too passive, Lord. I've lied, to tell you the truth. Please forgive my sin of lying and remind me clearly when I start to do it again. You know, Lord, this could be the beginning of something NEW! I'm a little scared, but excited, too!"

— 12 —

When Winter Comes

It has happened again, and you hoped it wouldn't. A curtain of ice has dropped between you and your husband, and you aren't sure how to melt it. You're not even sure you want to. He *deserves* to be left out in the cold. He's asked for it. But you're not sure he even minds.

For weeks you've felt the cool kisses, the frigid air when you "interrupt" his life with a question, a comment, a veiled play for a little attention.

At first, you could take it, but more and more you feel like a piece of furniture. Invisible. You may as well be his sister, or mother. . .or maid. And you ask yourself, "*This* is love?"

The words between you are clipped, functional, far apart. You miss the intimacy—the affection—and reach out in ways he doesn't notice. Maybe he's fighting his way out of a corner, and it's sapping his strength. Whatever it is, it's hard for him just now, and you know it. It's written all over him. Tired. Quiet. Sober. Unresponsive. Unfun.

But where does this leave you? You feel like an intruder. . .on the outside looking in. . .a visitor in your own backyard. You wonder how long it will go on. And you pray. A release valve opens, and you cry pent up tears. You feel better, but the talk button is unplugged. You want to look him in the eye and yell, "It's me! I'm your wife! Do you love me?" But pride locks the words inside and icicles keep forming.

Anger boils. . .seethes. Self-pity takes over. Pride joins the party.

When will it end? *Will* it end? Is this the beginning of the end? Is there anything you can do?

You grab a pen and start to write, "Dear _____, Where have you gone? I've missed you." You tell him exactly how you feel. Funny, it's easier this way. You consider leaving it where he'll get it. . . anticipating his response. Will he be shocked? Sorry? Angry? You look it over after an hour and strike out the accusing phrases. You read it again, and notice that you feel better. It's hours before he will see it. You read it later, and tone down the language a little more. It's almost as if you've talked it out with him. Then, later, before he sees it, you tear it up. And you pray, again.

It has helped. It is a beginning. You've looked at life from his perspective while you were waiting and decided to be the giver instead of the taker for this period. You'll ride out the wave, wait for the sun to shine. And you'll talk, somehow. You'll tell him you understand, that you miss him, but that you'll stay in the boat with him.

After all, he will have waves to ride out with you. He's already ridden plenty of them.

Then the ice begins to melt—in your heart. . .and very soon in his. Once again, the sun comes out from behind the cloud. And it is good.

Biblical Principle:
Marriage is a lifetime commitment to the good, the poor, the weak, the bad, the exciting.

My Scripture:
"For this reason a man will leave his father and mother and be united to his wife, and they will become one flesh" (Genesis 2:24, NIV).

My Prayer:
"Precious Lord, if a season of coldness creeps into my marriage, give me your power to ride out the storm, to keep on loving him, and to wait in the wings until the sun shines again. And, Lord, help me not to be the reason for his coldness. Keep the eyes of my heart always open to the commitment I made to him—and to you. Thank you, in Jesus' powerful name."

— 13 —
When Nothing Seems To Change

Why is it so easy to obey God when we see instant results? Why is it so hard when we have to wait—when we just have to put one foot ahead of the other with no relief in sight?

Karen* has been married to Fred* almost 17 years. They share four children, a home, and a church. Fred faithfully provides food, shelter, and clothing for the family. He is not a cruel man—except verbally. He attends church regularly with the family and often quotes Bible verses to his children—when correcting them. All in all—from the outside looking in—things don't look too bad. But Fred is spiritually stagnant. His faith is bloodless, without life and meaning when it comes to everyday living. What he knows he doesn't apply or use. His marriage has grown icy to the point of breaking. His children are alienated from him and almost from God because of his example in the home, in spite of the fact that they attend a Christian school. This head of the home, this God-appointed spiritual leader, has not led well. In many areas he has not led at

(*Names have been changed.)

71

all. And his family is struggling, suffering.

Karen has a growing and vital faith which she lives out in her home to the best of her ability. Every day she sits across the table from a husband who *will not change*. That is, a husband who will not surrender his life to Christ as Lord. He has made the right moves, but could not ever be convicted of being a Christian from his actions. There is no evidence of life. Many would wonder if he knows Christ as Savior.

His wife and his children have grappled with hope, despair, then more hope. Through her journey, Karen has become stronger and more secure in Christ, an able helper to many other women. But she lives with pain.

Karen shared what God is teaching her about living well in spite of a husband who does not change.

These life principles keep her going.

- Surrender to the Lord every day. Ask Him to make you exactly who and what He wants you to be. Allow Him to use you in your husband's life, to be the wife God wants you to be. Be such an example to him that he'll not be able to blame *you* for *his* refusal to be what he should be.
- Have a searching, willing attitude and heart.
- Develop friendships with other women, both those who share your situation and those who don't. From these, you can receive wise counsel, love, fellowship, emotional acceptance, and understanding. Don't have just one friend, but many. Broaden your perspective and horizons. Choose friends who will sympathize yet encourage and confront.
- Have "Aaron and Hur" prayer partners—ones who will hold you up and intercede for you.
- Lean into the sufficiency of God's grace during suffering. He is "Lord of the valleys," too. Immerse

yourself in Him.

- As you pray, name and fight against the spirit of despair, discouragement, depression, etc. These are individual attacks of the agents of Satan to be recognized as such and rebuked in the name of Jesus.
- Try to see the situation from God's perspective, not yours.
- Walk uprightly in spirit and true godliness.
- Don't condemn his spiritual walk.
- Don't be proud of your spiritual walk.

God may be using the other person to change *you*. He knows exactly what kind of mate will expose *your* faults so He can deal with them, too.

- Make the commitment to love without having to "feel."
- Be willing to obey Jesus even when it doesn't seem "fair." He will flow through an open heart.
- Don't let ministry to others come before ministry to your husband. No one has the opportunity to encourage him the way you do.
- Forgiveness is essential (daily!)
- Praise him in whatever ways you can.
- Learn to major on the majors. Learn to distinguish majors from minors.
- If you married the wrong person, realize he's the right one now, because you are married.
- Don't pray that the trial will end, but rather that God will use it to accomplish His purposes for the lives of all involved.
- Desire the Lord's will and the ultimate furtherance of His Kingdom more than you desire a "happy relationship" with your husband. Desire *His* love more than his love.
- Commit yourself to following Christ consistently,

no matter what the outcome of your situation.
- Don't demand that the Lord change your situation. God's best is known by surrender—not struggle.
- Allow God to use your husband and your situation to change you. Don't turn on the very things and people called of God into your life to change *you*.
- Remember you are not responsible for your husband's spiritual growth. You are responsible to the Lord for yours.
- Don't excuse yourself and become lazy spiritually.
- You *must* find ways to grow in the Lord.
- Recognize that fulfillment does not come from your wife role but from who you are in Christ.
- Never be sorry for feeling the hurt. Don't apologize. God understands.
- Give your children to the Lord in daily surrender and prayer. Allow Him to use this situation to touch them and enable them to grow, too.
- Submit to the Lord, but don't resign yourself to the situation and believe it will *never* change. Submit hopefully and prayerfully. Submission is active; resignation is passive.
- Work with and believe God's will—not the worldly probabilities. Don't listen to false counselors.

Biblical Principle:
God is still in control of the world and us no matter how things appear.

My Scripture:
"Since everything will be destroyed in this way, what

kind of people ought you to be? You ought to live holy and godly lives. . . .So then, dear friends, since you are looking forward to this, make every effort to be found spotless, blameless and at peace with him" (II Peter 3:11,14, NIV).

My Prayer:
"You are my God, my King, my Master. Help me not to lose sight of your power when I wonder how I can do it. All these things elude me—but you're here, aren't you? You can make it turn out right. . .even if it's me that needs correcting. Here goes, Lord: Take this whole frustrating part of my marriage and do whatever is best. Take it all—take it now. My soul follows hard after you. . . .I will trust and not be afraid."

— 14 —
Same Song, Different Verse

Are you and your husband on the same wavelength spiritually? If you are, you are highly and unusually blessed. Most Christian couples are on two separate journeys where growth and spiritual maturity is concerned. They find themselves see-sawing: First one is on a mountaintop, then the other. So what's a wife to do? Especially if she's running way out in front?

Don't Play God
Begin by recognizing spiritual growth as God's business—not yours or your husband's. God is in charge of you, *and* He is in charge of your husband. You are not responsible for *his* spiritual growth. You *are* responsible to obey God's Word. You *are* responsible to love, honor, submit, respect, and pray for your husband. And our God, who can be fully trusted to keep His word, will somehow, some way, and in His time, honor your obedience.

Spiritual maturity is a result of obeying God. Be assured, there is no shortcut, no other way to authentic growth. And you can't make your husband obey God because obedience is a door marked "private" in each of us.

Yes, the Lord does want our husbands to obey Him, too, but He won't invade the sanctuary of their will and *make* them obey. God has a vast, unexplainable respect for the human will. He will influence, draw, convict, woo, and wait. But He will not go where He is not invited.

If you have been over-anxious about your husband's lack of spiritual growth, take a deep breath right now and relax your worry into God's hands. Remember whose work it is to draw your husband into fuller obedience to Him.

Perhaps our most significant contribution to our husbands' spiritual maturity is to obey God ourselves in the ways we respond to our husbands. First Corinthians 7:14 says plainly, "For the unbelieving husband has been sanctified through his wife." This passage addresses wives and husbands who have unbelieving spouses, but the principle also applies to husbands who aren't living what they say they believe. As a wife we can have a powerful and positive spiritual influence simply by obeying God ourselves.

Quite honestly, because of our nurturing nature, we wives turn all too quickly to nagging and maneuvering our husbands into an unnatural obedience which is nothing short of ridiculous. It never works, and only adds boulders to his wall of resistance. We cannot coerce our husbands into a closer walk with God. We can obey, wait, and pray in the calm assurance that God's Holy Spirit will work in the right time, *His* time, His way.

We can also:

(1) Establish a support group of believing wives in

the same situation.

(2) Have a prayer partner, not to share criticisms with, but to intercede with you.

Look In The Mirror

If you seem to be way out in front of your husband spiritually, ask yourself why you feel that way. Who told you you were? What list are you using to judge your husband? Are you quite sure your spiritual perception is unclouded and free of a critical, demanding spirit? Or, is the log in your own eye so large you can't see the splinter in your husband's clearly? If you look inside yourself and find a lot of non-acceptance and resentment, you and God have some work to do—on you!

There are wives who keep "lists." There are scores of thing they *don't* do and places they *don't* go, and their attitudes at home toward their husbands are destructive and judgmental. These wives do not demonstrate an authentic growing faith. And the husbands they constantly condemn are sometimes, under their skin, growing Christians. Setting ourselves up as judge, jury, and chief nagger muddies our perceptions.

When you perceive yourself to be "out ahead," it is easy to be consumed by the sin of spiritual pride and not even realize it. You're certain he will never "catch up" to you. Interestingly, God expects Christians to grow, but He condemns spiritual pride. Proverbs 6:16–19 and I Timothy 8:6 tell us He hates pride. A prideful, holier-than-thou attitude from a wife will alienate any husband, not draw him to a closer walk. As ambassadors of God, we must represent Him through a godly lifestyle, conversation, actions.

If you dare, ask God to show you *your* heart and to give you eyes to see and repent where need be. One lovely Christian wife I know found a new, sweet release to enjoy her husband when she confessed her resentment. Christianity *is* practical!

If we are genuinely close in our walk with the Lord, we will have an accepting attitude toward our husbands. Our attitude will say by its actions, "I accept you as you are." "I like you just they way you are." Did I hear a gulp? This doesn't mean we throw away our good and earnest desire for him to draw closer to the Lord. No, only that we give our desire to the One who is able to fulfill it: Jesus Christ, the Son of the living God. It's His job to change people, not ours.

Not accepting our husbands is disobedience to God's clear directive to wives in I Peter 3. "Wives, in the same way be submissive to your husbands so that, if any of them do not believe the word, they may be won over without talk by the behavior of their wives, when they see the purity and reverence of your lives. Your beauty. . .should be that of your inner self, the unfading beauty of a gentle and quiet spirit, which is of great worth in God's sight."

Did you notice that phrase, "that they may be won over *without talk!*" Non-acceptance must be acknowledged as sin and dealt with by repentance. In other words, confessed and forsaken. Otherwise it will leak like a poison into mealtimes, recreation times, discussions, and will even be an unwelcome intruder in the marriage bed. It festers and grows like an infected wound left undressed unless it's brought to the cross. . . daily if need be.

Clearly, the God we meet in the Bible accepts *us* where we come from and helps us along the way to where He wants us to go. If *we* can't accept our husbands, and we are their link to Christianity, how can he possibly believe in a God who will unconditionally accept him? We represent God in a very earthly sense. The closer we walk with God, the more unconditionally we will be able to accept our husbands' spiritual condition. Kind of like the way God accepts us in Romans 5:8.

Non-acceptance is a huge stumbling block in the way of anyone's spiritual growth. Let's take the matter of prayer. To continually share answers to prayer with a husband who doesn't pray is a slap in his face. It can also be a manipulative device on the part of the wife who is, in essence, saying, "If you would pray, you would get these kinds of answers, too." Words don't always need to be spoken in order to communicate. Every time you give glowing accounts of answered prayer to someone who doesn't pray, they feel defensive or guilty. It punches a hole in their balloon. But it doesn't necessarily encourage them to pray.

Wisdom would share those answers to prayer with a friend who would understand and rejoice with you. Wisdom would be selective in answers shared with a non-believing or spiritually immature husband.

One wife forced her husband to take the lead in family devotions when the poor man, at this stage, was embarrassed and uncomfortable and balked at the idea. To keep the peace, he did make a feeble stab at devotions for awhile, but they were forced, staged, erratic, and basically unproductive. Usually, by the time "devotions" were ended, the family members were tense and angry at each other, or they slept through it. She was ready *NOW* for the ideal husband, but she wasn't willing to wait for God to develop him.

Jesus says, "Love each other as I have loved you" (John 15:12). Take a look at Jesus' kind of love. It's unconditional. He loves us warts and all. His love is forgiving and healing. It's accepting. He doesn't even *remember* the sins we have confessed and keep wanting to dredge up (Psalm 103:12). His love draws and nurtures, He attracts our obedience and our love by what He offers. His love is self-sacrificing. He left heaven for a human life and a human death on this sin-cursed earth. His love gave *all*.

Jesus can develop this kind of winsome, attractive love in us for our husbands if we ask Him and allow Him to do so. Love has such a wonderful way of transforming husbands from the inside out. You may not even recognize yourself!

Adapt To Him

"Wives. . .be submissive to your husbands so that, if any of them do not believe the word they may be won over without words by the behavior of their wives" (I Peter 3:1, NIV).

Another word for submissive, used in a paraphrase is adapt, a dusty, mostly unused word. Much like the word submission, it has been ignored and laughed at, scorned and buried in the attics of our brains, labeled impractical at the least and ridiculous at best. Five letters—and a concept so big and so far reaching it stretches around the globe.

Do only wimpy wives adapt? No. It takes tremendous strength of character to decide to obey God when it *looks* like He's going to take our toys away. It takes courage. It's the choice of strength. It's the hard choice of obedience. But what does adapt really mean when all the dust is blown away?

One slice of the word "adapt" means to *modify* ourselves and our plans to fit alongside our husband's plans. It means to choose to live in a complementary fashion as much as possible. It means to accommodate, to make room for, to allow for, to adjust

81

ourselves and *our* plans. It means we are to *cooperate* rather than *compete* with our husband's life.

A word of caution here. Our delightful Lord is a God of common sense and love who doesn't order us to join our husbands in illegal or immoral activities. He doesn't force you to join your husband at events which deeply offend your conscience or God's Word. He simply urges you and me to make reasonable and earnest efforts to adapt rather than to resist stubbornly. Adapting to your husband is even more important than adapting to an employer. Employers fade away, but husbands are not dispensable.

In a very real sense, marriage is a career choice, no matter what else you may do. It is a pair of individuals who have decided to wend their way through life together, come what may. And both partners can't be number one. Someone must adapt, and the only clear order scripturally to do just that is given to the wife. I don't believe that means the husband is never to adapt, and I don't think God had that in mind because He said husbands are to love their wives as Christ loved the church (Ephesians 5:25). And that's a pretty sacrificial kind of love! But because He knew we wives would be resistant to adapting, He put special emphasis on the importance of it.

Edith Schaeffer, wife of renowned Christian leader Francis Schaeffer (now deceased) has said, "Someone must adapt, and I, for one, am willing." Many times adapting will take a decisive and powerful restraint on your part. It is a decision forged out of great strength—not weakness.

The joy of this directive to wives to adapt is that wives don't need to accept the final responsibility for decisions. My friend, Carol Currey, succinctly says, "Why not obey God? I have nothing to lose and everything to gain." Her family life is an example of the happiness God means for us all to have. She and her husband have *dared* to obey God and have reaped a fun-filled, godly home that scatters sunshine on all who enter.

Adapting creates a resting place for wives. So many women I know suffer needless and chronic anxiety because they can't nestle down into this resting place provided by God for women. They *must* take charge, at work *and* at home. They insist that their husbands adapt to them. Or they pretend to adapt, but rebel and fret endlessly instead of resting. This is backward, upside down living, and it's happening all around us.

This will raise the question of church attendance and ministry for some wives. If you have a husband who *demands* that you not attend church, some would say, "Oppose him." Some would say, "Don't go at all." May I suggest you look for a way to adapt to what he seems to need from you and look for a way to worship with others at the same time? It may mean staying home on Sunday morning, but worshiping in a small group of believers at another time. If your church doesn't have small groups, pray about starting one. You could begin by meeting at a time your husband won't be disturbed or annoyed. Through prayer, seek guidance for workable worship.

Ministry overdone can actually hinder a husband's spiritual growth. If you are over-busy and neglect his needs, you need to drop back until his needs are met reasonably. I believe our homes are to be the primary place of ministry, no matter what else may command our attention. After you are married, your husband is your primary earthly commitment, no matter what else calls for attention. And if true ministry—service to others—doesn't begin at home, it can only be a counter-feit elsewhere.

Ministry can be a monster eating away at the doors of your tent. One wife paid monstrous babysitting bills every month so she could attend *all* the services of her church. Her home was in a turmoil of problems; her house was unkempt to the point of shamefulness, and her pocketbook was empty. . .until the Lord lovingly opened her eyes.

Adapt. It is a magical, mysterious word. It calls for all the courage and tact we can muster.

Respect Him

One of a husband's primary needs is to be respected by his wife. Respect is such a little word, but is one giant principle to capture in truth. If you read Scripture, love going to church, receive answers to prayer, minister actively, and are growing in the Lord, you may find yourself respecting *yourself* or *other Christians* much more than you respect your husband. And when you build up *others* in his presence, you subtly tear down his sense of importance. Down deep inside, he will feel what you are really saying and resent it. He will understand you to say you really respect others more than him and wish he would get his act together because he doesn't quite make it with you.

Refrain from talking about "wonderful" sermons you heard, or the "deep spirituality" of someone else's husband. He *knows* he doesn't measure up already. And when he sees how you admire other men he may retreat into silence or some other diversionary tactic. Then you'll wonder where he went emotionally.

First Peter 3 says to acknowledge the headship of *our* husband—not someone else's. Find ways to let *your* husband know what you respect about him. Ask his opinion about things, letting him know you appreciate and turn to him. But even in this, don't pretend or manipulate. Just be sincere. There *are* things he's good at—things he knows more about than you. Tap into his knowledge and build your marriage in the process.

Discuss matters with him rather than some "expert" whenever possible. Glean any wisdom from him you can find, and tell him how much you truly appreciate and need *his* insights.

Find things to praise and admire about your husband. These kinds of loving acts translate into respect from his perspective.

Is he faithful about going to work? Respect that faithfulness, and tell him so. Does he let you decorate your home without interfering? Let him know you think that's great. Is he neat? Is he polite? Is he honest? Look your husband over from head to toe and find everything about him you possibly can, then admire it with an enthusiasm that never ends!

Mary is a wife who has just cause to be deeply disappointed in her Christian husband, yet she appreciates the freedom he gives her not to work outside the home and to be a full-time mother. She uses her discretionary time to minister to hurting women all over her community in a myriad of ways. She lets her husband know she appreciates that particular freedom.

Our God, who designed marriage, knows these actions of admiration, praise, and devotion communicate respect and are a dynamic ingredient in any marriage. Unfortunately, they seem to be foreign, musty words, even in Christendom. But so are marriages that last and *are happy.*

To push and shove and demand and manipulate within marrige is to trample on its delicate fabric with muddy boots, then expect it to remain a pure, expensive garment of great price. These types of actions demonstrate a lack of respect and reveal a personal sin problem that needs emergency care.

On our road to truly and sincerely respecting our husbands, we must look for times we can honestly *defer to their* judgment on a matter. "You're right, honey." "I haven't seen it that way before." "Good thought." "Thanks for helping me understand." These words are the oil of gladness to any marriage.

Find ways to *need* your husband's help or advice. Let him know you value his judgment and expertise on *something*. When he understands he is actually, genuinely valued, it releases in him the personal freedom to relax and be himself, to know that it's okay to fail once in awhile. He will feel—and relax in—the freedom of being loved for who he is. Also, it makes you more womanly and appealing in his eys. There is something in a man's make up which rather enjoys the occasional "helplessness" of a woman (especially if he can do something she can't do!). It usually delights a man to exert his manliness or his strength no matter what the occasion, and he deserves the opportunity.

Perhaps one of the most effective and challenging ways to show respect for a husband is to trust him to be able to provide for you. Men are natural providers if allowed to be, and if the time comes when he can't, help him move gracefully through the crisis without condemnation. Ordinarily, men enjoy working and their identity is wrapped up in their work (much more so than a woman's), so when they are deprived of work, they feel a very real loss of identity and purpose. To understand this is to be a helpmate of great worth.

The issue is respect. *Whatever* we do, whatever happens in the course of living and loving, our focus as Christian wives must be to show respect for our husbands. They must have it, just as we must have affection in order to really "bloom" and enjoy our marriages.

My husband and I have a friend who has suffered several reversals on the way to financial freedom. At times, he and his wife were (to others at least) destitute for short periods as he developed work in line with his unique abilities for promotion. His wife, in every case, has stood beside him, supporting and respecting his abilities—not behind him pushing and maneuvering and afraid. She has encouraged, adapted, praised, and helped him find his way even when it was dark. She has adapted when things were lean, and now that money is not a problem, she also adapts. He is still her provider, and he has grown in line with her trust. He never fails to refer to her with delight, praising her ability to motivate him by respecting him. Like the passage in I Peter 3:4, she has the unfading charm of a gentle and peaceful spirit which is not anxious or wrought up.

Brag, Don't Nag

In the description of the Proverbs 31 woman, we read, "She opens her mouth in wisdom, and the teaching of kindness is on her tongue" (31:25). The Song of Solomon is filled with personal descriptions of praise and appreciation for the bride's husband. Chapter 5 gives the maiden's answer to her friends when they ask what kind of beloved her husband is. "My beloved is dazzling and ruddy, outstanding among ten thousand" (5:10).

Godly women appreciate and prize their husbands. It never hurts to brag about his accomplishments, to uphold him in public as well as private. As the old saying goes, "It's a poor duck that doesn't praise its own pond." It's a poor wife who doesn't praise her own husband.

Wives have a responsibility to the home, the family unit, the children, and their husbands. When we uphold our husbands in the family circle, our children know we are loyal to their father, that he's important. Loyalty is a much-prized virtue—in business or in the home. Defend your husband. Stand up for him. Never, never, never cut him down in front of his friends, your friends, or your children.

The ongoing work of marriage is to build up one another, not tear down. Your husband is like any man—he will not be interested in a faith which acts itself out by critical condemnation, spoken or unspoken.

Nagging is nothing more or less than demanding that your husband make you happy by scurrying to meet *your* criteria for happiness. I know, because I have done it. To husbands, nagging is highly unattractive, or, to put it more bluntly, ugly. It drives them away. Nagging is like a dripping faucet in the dark of the night, or as Proverbs says, "It is better to dwell in the wilderness, than with a contentious and an angry woman" (21:19, KJV). Or, "A constant dripping on a day of steady rain and a contentious woman are alike" (27:15, NASB). Nagging wives drive men away from their families and their God. It forces them to either retreat or fight to preserve their dignity.

Love, on the other hand, draws, nurtures, and brags wherever possible. Love is winsome—the fragrant perfume of marriage.

Respect, defer to, honor, esteem, appreciate, prize, adore, admire, praise, be devoted to, deeply love and enjoy, follow his lead. . .all of these are the heavenly words of life to a growing marriage.

These are the keys to personal honor, happiness,

and to your husband's spiritual life, also. And they are in *OUR HANDS*. . .on our tongues.

Show, Don't Tell

Husbands don't care so much about what we say or even what we believe. They may not care what the preacher says or what the Bible says. But he *will* care about what our life says. Our actions leave a trail of unspoken words day and night. Our lives are a manuscript in motion, a Bible with legs and a mouth. Every day and every night we write a new chapter in our marriages. Is it good reading?

Telling about God or the Bible seldom if ever draws a husband into a closer walk with the Lord. *Living* often does. Sometimes talking about your faith, whether victories or defeats, becomes spiritual one-upmanship. It comes off as bragging or insinuation, but living your faith shows what you believe and how it works.

Telling about your faith can diminish his sense of worthiness which may even result in some defensive lashing out on his part. *Show* the gospel. *Live* the gospel. *Love* the Lord and enjoy Him, but leave your husband up to the Lord who loves him even more than you do. God is patient and longsuffering.

Biblical Principle:
Winsome, tactful wifery will encourage a husband to a closer walk with Christ far better than a lot of talk.

My Scripture:
"An excellent wife is the crown of her husband, but she who shames him is as rottenness in his bones" (Proverbs 12:4, NASB).

My Prayer:

"Oh, Lord! This is such a big order. You've got an awful lot of work to do in me, haven't you? I don't *want* to do these things! It goes against my grain so badly I can't tell you. But you know anyway, don't you. Maybe that's why I keep running into blank walls. I've played the "blame game" long enough. Maybe it's time to try your game plan. . . .Holy Spirit of God, work in me."

Part 3

Living in the world of work—sometimes it's a pain, sometimes a delight, but it always needs a sensitive heart to know the will of God and to encourage the heart of a husband/provider.

— 15 —
Your Husband At Work

Work. No matter how much we complain about it, moan about it, gripe about it, it *is* honorable. It *is* profitable (most of the time!) It *is* biblical. Kept in perspective with rest, it is good. God talks about it in several places in Scripture:

- "If a man will not work, he shall not eat" (II Thessalonians 3:10, NIV).
- "So I saw that there is nothing better for a man than to enjoy his work, because that is his lot" (Ecclesiastes 3:22, NIV).
- "You shall work six days, but on the seventh day you shall rest; even during plowing time and harvest you shall rest" (Exodus 34:21, NASB).
- "He also who is slack in his work is brother to him who destroys" (Proverbs 18:9, NASB).

God wants us to enjoy our work. He planned, in the beginning, for work to satisfy perfectly. Adam's first recorded work assignment was to "dress" and "keep" the Garden of Eden. He was to care for the magnificent trees throughout the garden. At this time, perfection crowned the earth, including perfect satisfaction in

93

labor. But after sin, the ground was cursed (Genesis 3:17-19), and God told Adam plainly and unmistakably that his future toil would have more than its share of pain and sweat as well as thorns and thistles. Pure pleasure in working was gone.

Why say this? Because our husbands are "Adam" many times removed. He is "Adam" in nature and in response to his work (as well as other things). And it is this nature within him we need to understand in order to support him when life gets sticky in the castle.

Take a trip with me into the inner sanctuary of our husbands, and let's look at some characteristics of the way he works.

He Is Work Oriented

Generally speaking, the man in your life will be what we call "team loyal" to his work. The same man who will "kill" to get to work on time may think nothing of coming in late for your once-hot meal. He may not even understand why you are angry, or the meal is cold. Something in his male insides pulls strongly toward his work or occupation, especially if he really enjoys what he is doing.

The Down Side: For you, this could mean lots of frustration because you see him "moving away" emotionally or physically. You may find yourself pulling all kinds of strings to fence him in at least a *little* more. And your pulling could easily move into demanding or nagging. Accusations and misunderstanding could pile up until alienation sets in, which is the last thing you want.

The Up Side: Someone, at least, in a team of two, *must* feel strongly responsible for earning a living, or it won't happen at all. I believe God has beautifully fitted men with an instinctive urge or drive to provide in order to insure provision for the families He gives them. We can be thankful for that.

Our Father God, the Ultimate Provider, feels strongly enough about the matter of provision to include these words in the eternal ink of Scripture: "If anyone does not provide for his relatives, and especially for his immediate family, he has denied the faith and is worse than an unbeliever" (I Timothy 5:8, NIV).

Our Response: We can thank God if our husbands are strong providers. We can tell our husbands how much we appreciate his sense of responsibility and his provision *no matter how small the dollar amount.* We can facilitate his work rather than balk against it. We can and must also be frank, but not accusing, when he is off balance and gives *too* much time and energy to his work. This concern might be expressed something like this:

"Honey, I'm missing you lately. I feel sort of left out of your life, like you have no time or interest in our being together. Could we talk about it?"

Don't wait years for a discussion like this. Some husbands may need a wifely nudge every few weeks—*before* emotional separation and dryness set in.

He Works In a Society At War

The unbelieving world system is openly at war with Christ-centered values. On the job, your husband may be in front line battle every day between his conscience or faith and the corporate culture. He may often come home wounded. In the back of his head, the messages of the secular power gurus are telling him, "Win at any cost. You've got to do these things to get ahead." Brashness, aggressiveness, and using or manipulating others for personal gain dominate many work places. Working daily on the edge of dismissal, trying to look better than the other guy just to keep his job, the battle zone fills with silent screams.

Men are being brutally pitted against each other. And men must choose whom they will follow.

For the Christian, this philosophy simply does not fly. It's nothing more than an age-old lie from the father of lies who has remodeled and reshaped it to fit our age. But underneath all the new words is a putrifying stench—a trap covered over with beautiful green leaves, or appealing, forbidden fruit.

The Down Side: Men (and their families) are drowning in the flood of magazine articles and seminars teaching people to bare their teeth, growl, and, if necessary, devour each other for dinner. . .just to "get ahead."

Your husband may work in this kind of pressure-cooker environment. (And today, so may you.) It may be a constant balancing act for him to live out Christian principles at work. Because of the restrictions of the workplace, he may wait until he gets home to let off steam.

The Up Side: Light always shines brightest where it is dark. A man who lives by Christian principles *will* shine against this dark backdrop, becoming salt and light to the soul-hungry around him.

Our Response: Don't be party to the group pushing your husband to the brink of exhaustion—the group encouraging him to seek power and money. Promotion may come. So may power and money. But none of these are the goal. To live for Christ is always the Christian's goal. And if, in the process of doing business in a Christ-like manner, God chooses to bless in these ways, let it be received with humility and given back in ways that will glorify Him.

Ask God to purify your own motives in wanting to "get ahead." Ask yourself "why" you want more money, a bigger house, a nicer car (if you do), and who it will glorify. Be the godly "balancer" your husband needs.

He Is Competitive
Many husbands keenly enjoy the boxing ring atmosphere of the workplace. They like putting on their gloves and stepping into the ring each morning. The challenge stimulates them—makes the creative juices flow. This is a good, healthy kind of ambition and can help him be a diligent worker. If "competitive" describes your husband, here is:

The Up Side: He will probably be more interesting to live with than someone who has no motivation at all. Life will probably be full of challenges and, hopefully, fun as you ride the roller coaster together. At least he *is* motivated. He *is* alive.

The Down Side: A runaway competitive spirit can easily consume a good man and become a personal rivalry between him and every man he meets. Jerry and Mary White put it well in their book *Your Job, Survival Or Satisfaction?* when they say, "When the goal changes from doing an excellent job to "beating out" another person, competition has become unhealthy ambition." They state further, "We should compete against a *standard*, not a person."

Our Response: Pray that God will give you *both* a keen and discerning spirit so you can sense when competition has done a flip-flop and become a rivalry between him and his co-workers or friends.

If he enjoys reading, there are several books written to Christian men about work. But over and above them all is Scripture which contains all the wisdom he will ever need.

Don't expect life to be dull or without challenges. He may be a man who gets promotions often. It may mean moving frequently. Wives in this situation need to be flexible and adaptable. They need to become women of prayer.

If your husband is not strongly grounded in Scripture, he may easily believe Satan's lie that it doesn't pay to live and work by Christian principles. If he has bought into the world's philosophy, he may be very stressed and less lovable than if he relaxed into God's truths. He may be less affectionate, and you may get secondhand, warmed-over, leftover love. He may find it hard to switch gears when he gets home and continue to compete with you. He may just push *you* to the edge.

In a *Detroit News*, April 27, 1989, article, Robin Abcarian advised accepting positions because of their *power* potential, not *turning down* positions because of what they may do to relationships.

If your husband is caught in this kind of information web and believes it, tell him you're concerned about *him* as well as what it can do to your relationship. You might suggest a Bible study together on biblical workstyles and attitudes. God's Word is always a lamp to our feet and a light to our path (Psalm 119:105). Look to Him for wisdom and guidance.

God Is His Provider

One of the names of God is Jehovah-Jireh, The God Who Will Provide (Genesis 22:13-14).

God has promised to supply all your husband's needs (Philippians 4:19). He is your husband's primary caregiver—his source of income—his means of provision. Whether or not he ever receives another check from an employer, God will provide for his needs (and yours) because He is bound by His own Word. Most of us have never really believed and tested God in this way. But Hudson Taylor did. George Mueller did. Others have and are. They each discovered a God who keeps His word.

It's both exciting and a little scary to believe God in this way, but we can learn to look *way* past a paycheck for provision. We can learn to look *way* past our husband or our own job for provision. Sometimes it is a blessing to be "up against it." That is exactly where God steps in and keeps His word. At the end of our flimsy, man-made ropes, we find God.

Lift up your eyes and see the very heart and hand of a God who provides.

More than being just some frilly words to fill up a page, this kind of trusting has been put to the test in my own life during the past five years. We have looked God's promise full in the face and found a Lord who isn't in any kind of financial distress whatsoever. Here's our story:

After 20 years in the ivy-covered walls of education, my husband stepped into the mysterious waters of going into business independently. Very independently. He became a carpenter. Oh, he already had the skill, the licensing, and the strong interest. He also had a healthy amount of practical experience. It was a sensible choice in many ways.

We knew we were in for a new lifestyle. There would be no regular paycheck. And when the paycheck came, the amount would be different all the time. And there was no promise of a paycheck at all if he couldn't find jobs.

He decided not to advertise at all. Not even a business card. He simply put the word out that this was what he was available to do from now on among friends and associates. We prayed. And we waited.

From the last day he worked at a local Christian

college until this day, he has not been without work for one day. But many, many times, he has not known from one week to the next or one day to the next, if there would be work. It has always come. To us this is a small but wonderful miracle.

It is our mutual decision that I not work full-time at paid employment, so I was not under pressure to be his provider when no work appeared to be coming. I *was* pledged to pray for him. Another part of my work was to "earn money by not spending it unnecessarily." The most important part of my work, according to Roy, was to completely trust both him and God to provide without worrying or nagging. We discovered that my confidence in him gave him confidence in both himself and the Lord. My position was this: If God wasn't going to worry, and Roy wasn't going to worry, I *sure* wasn't going to worry!

The annual income? In case you're thinking otherwise, it has been hovering around $22,000 for the three of us, and for awhile there were four. Yet, we have so much more than we need.

This is a personal experience, yes. But God doesn't limit His promises of provision to one couple or circumstance. *We* limit His promises by not believing them.

For us, this one promise, this characteristic of our great God, has meant *so* much to our total lifestyle and sense of well-being. It has been a unique experience, because we, too, were firmly entrenched in trusting a paycheck and an employer.

I don't urge you to imitate our experience. I do urge you to trust our Almighty Provider in your particular circumstance in a greater way. And I urge you to trust your husband and encourage him by your trust.

If you feel your circumstances are "special," you may

want to discuss these principles with your pastor or a trusted Christian friend. But really trusting *God* to be our provider is the kind of Christianity that hits the pavement daily and paints a grin on our faces and puts a twinkle in our eyes.

Why do we have all we need and then some?

First Timothy 6:15 says not to fix our hope "on the uncertainty of riches, but on God, who richly supplies us with all things to enjoy." And even if He doesn't give us the nice "things" we want (covet), He is still a *good* God because He always knows what we really need (which sometimes is a little hardship!).

Where are you and your husband? Wherever it is, God knows, cares, and will keep His promises.

Biblical Principle:

Work is God ordained and produces satisfaction. Whatever God gives us to do, we should trust Him to provide.

My Scripture:

"A man can do nothing better than to eat and drink and find satisfaction in his work. This too, I see, is from the hand of God, for without him, who can eat or find enjoyment?" (Ecclesiastes 2:24–25, NIV)

"I know that there is nothing better for them than to rejoice and to do good in one's lifetime, moreover, that every man who eats and drinks sees good in all his labor—it is the gift of God" (Ecclesiastes 3:12–13, NASB).

My Prayer:

"You mean I don't have to worry so much about his work or our income? What a relief that would be.

101

Father, is Christianity really this practical? You. . .the Provider. I like that picture. Teach me the fullness of this truth, because, frankly, I haven't lived like you were in charge of this at all. It's time to begin."

— 16 —
A Story About Working

If you are one of the majority of wives who work outside the home (as well as inside!), you may glean a bit of help from one of my own experiences which occurred on the job several years ago. This incident relaxed an anxiety which was getting too big and boiling over into my marriage and family life. I share it because it is common for us all to have times of testing and unhappiness in our work, whether we're in the home or outside it. I also share it because God gave me a solution not often found in women's magazines or counseling offices. But then, aren't God's solutions often unusual—to say the least?

Life in my workplace was getting *very* hectic. Never, in my wildest dreams, had I imagined that in a matter of two short months I could change from a confident, competent worker who took pride in good work, to a virtual flunkie who felt like an invisible robot with a thousand arms, none of which could move fast enough. Surely I deserved better!

By a curious set of circumstances, temporarily beyond my control, I was suddenly expected to do the most menial work, twice as much of it as when I began the job, and faster than humanly possible (I thought).

To make it even worse, a younger and more inexperienced woman was given authority to parcel out this work to me, and I was steaming! What right did God (He always get the blame, doesn't He?) have to do this to me?

Fortunately, God was gracious with me, as usual, and through good counsel from my husband and friends, I saw the problem more clearly. The *problem* was not my problem. *My attitude* was the problem. I realized I couldn't necessarily expect circumstances to change, at least not immediately, but I could let the Lord change my responses to those circumstances. A few days later. . . .

I entered the office and looked around. Everything looked the same. Work was being conducted to harmonize with the furious inner rhythm of the success song my employer sang day and night. Typewriters hummed. Phones jangled. Mistakes caused general uproar. Everything was due yesterday. A stack of labels and names was dropped unceremoniously on my desk with a hurried thump, and a feminine voice said matter-of-factly, "He wants these done by 11 o'clock." This all happened before I had removed my coat or sat down.

I looked at the carrier of this good news, and saw that *she* hadn't changed. Not at all. But I could feel that *something* had changed.

I fingered the stack of work and missed the usual pang of resentment that went with it. Today, she only *thought* she was giving me the work. Today, I saw the work as coming directly from the loving hand of God.

A faint, new rhythm began to play around in my head as my hands addressed the labels. I hummed the unfamiliar tune and decided I liked it better than the old one. The grinding in my stomach slowly gave way to an insistent melody, and somehow it really didn't matter as much that, for a time at least, I was being overworked and under-appreciated. That could conceivably change in time, and I would make plans to speak to my employer as soon as reasonably possible to suggest an alternative work arrangement.

In the meantime, I had a new handle on the situation through Christ. I viewed every assignment as from Him. And it made a vast difference in how I perceived the work and how I did it.

Why do I say this? I think because I see the attitude about work and working as so important. Some things we will be able to change and should change. Others, we can't change. It's here that our attitude will make us or break our back.

All work has its dissatisfying parts. But even in the very middle of an unsatisfying "bog," we can experience the almost unnerving power of a responsive Savior working for good in our situation.

In this incident, I was able to respond in faith because I knew God well enough to know He loved me and was in charge of my character development. I knew He wasn't "out to get me." I was confident (and you can be, too) that He was working all events in my life together for my eventual good (Romans 8:28–29) to make me more like Him. My confidence came from the only source of truth about God and how He works in human lives: the Bible. Power, confidence, and eventual joy spring from an intimate friendship with the Savior. He allowed my experience primarily for my growth, and—He knew I would be sharing it with you.

As a Christian wife/worker, you have resources unknown to those outside Christ. You have all that Christ is. You don't have to do it all by yourself—in fact, you have probably already discovered that you can't. Herein lies your greatest strength: to realize your weakness and plug that very weakness into the power source of Christ's strength.

Make changes where you can, but try to accept those areas you cannot change as learning points allowed by Him to refine and purify your character. All of Scripture reverberates with the truth God loves us individually and is working with us individually and lovingly.

Your situation won't ever really be the whole problem, as it wasn't really mine. Your attitude will be the real problem in many instances. And fortunately, attitudes can be altered and influenced remarkably in some very practical ways.

I doubt if it's ever really possible to keep family life from spilling over into the workplace, or whether it's possible to prevent our life at work from spilling into our homes. Most of us are just not that compartmentalized. There will be problems and joys in both places. Perhaps the most important thing to remember, no matter what our situation, is that *we* can be altered.

My workplace was a "bog" for awhile, and I learned that only God can give a melody in the middle of a bog. It's a good song He plants in us—a sweet song—one composed in the heavenlies. He's waiting to teach it to you, too.

Biblical Principle:
God takes all situations in the life of a Christian and uses them for something good.

My Scripture:

"And we know that in all things God works for the good of those who love him, who have been called according to his purpose. For those God foreknew he also predestined to be conformed to the likeness of His Son. . . ." (Romans 8:28–29, NIV)

My Prayer:

"Okay, Lord. This is a big lump to swallow. I can hardly believe you are able to do this kind of thing. I thought it all depended on me and my strength and cleverness. But it doesn't. You know what I'm running into with my work. You know it's almost too much at times. Here it is, Lord. I don't want it any more. Change me in this circumstance and let others see you and your victory in my life."

— 17 —
Just Thinkin' About Workin'

It was coffee break time, and the hum of conversation rose and fell in the usual rhythms among my co-workers. The men compared golf scores and gas mileage. The women talked fashion and kids and home. As a temporary secretary on assignment I had heard it all before in other businesses. Everywhere I went, the married women in their spare moments were "at home in their heads." This was true no matter what their salary or position. I wondered why.

Why did so many women act so displaced? Why did the soft cocoon of a woman's heart turn so quickly and happily toward home? And why did so many of these apparently well-to-do women choose to work? It seemed by their conversations that they were really focused on their husbands and children. I listened. I read. I observed. And I learned.

I learned that sometimes a wife goes to work in addition to managing her home and family because she's looking for a solution: to loneliness, to unpaid bills, to overall dissatisfaction, or maybe to boredom.

From personal experience I knew that, sometimes, a

job or career can solve these problems to a degree. But only *if* the co-workers are congenial. Only *if* the paycheck is substantial. And only *if* the new boss throws more roses than lemons. But unfortunately, all of these benefits seldom come packaged in the same box. And there is a law of nature that seems to go something like this: Each new solution brings with it at least one new problem that itself needs a solution.

Take loneliness, for example. Co-workers *can* be great. But they can also tie you up in festering relational knots. And after we've used our freshest hours to deal with co-worker problems all day, the husband we come home to often gets little more than our leftovers in *every* way.

Quite naturally, our husbands turn to us first for understanding, sympathy, advice, encouragement. These are part of the things we pledge to him on our wedding day. And if we're burned out before we hit the door, where is he to turn? The brightest and best of our emotional and physical energies will go to *someone*.

Then, there's the problem of the yawning wallet. A paycheck in the palm *does* feel good. It's satisfying and comforting and secure. But there are the special clothes, the car, the babysitter, possibly the cost of hiring cleaning and yard work done. Then there are the lunch and coffee break treats, the gifts for others at the office—and the new tax bracket. There are new decisions about "my money and your money" and what's fair and what isn't. There's that "hungry" feeling to deal with when you want to spend "your" money and HE objects. A paycheck also has a curious way of shrinking faster than 100 percent cotton. Is the added money worth the cost to acquire it?

Let's talk about boredom for a minute. I've been bored when dressed in a let's-do-business suit and labeled Executive Secretary. I've been bored with the mundane details that accompany freelancing. And I've met those with impressive titles who also complain about boredom. Boredom is deadening, brain-stifling, thought-paralyzing, and just plain unhealthy. We don't want it or like it. But is "going to work" the answer? Or does boredom originate inside us rather than outside?

I wonder if, more often than not, boredom is not simply a state of mind. . .an inert spirit that needs to wake up to the soaring possibilities of meaningful existence God has for us. I wonder if boredom could be turned inside out and upside down by time spent on other people rather than on acquiring things? The happiest, most contented women I know consistently pour their lives into the lives of others in meaningful, helpful ways. They focus on being the hands of Jesus and ministering in the same ways He would.

Then, of course, a positive work environment can be tremendously reinforcing. It can give a sense of worth and self-esteem. Perhaps your husband isn't reinforcing you, and you could use some positive feedback more often. Well, quite frankly, this shortage occurs in even the best marriages sometimes. Reinforcement, when it comes from any source, is a shining, white-robed angel. But for many, or even most wives, it is an extra.

A godly, wise husband *will* show his gratitude for you and your work regularly and affectionately. But in the absence of this, it is possible to reinforce yourself. . . to believe in what you're doing and who you are. It is possible, by God's grace, to plant your feet firmly in your own garden and grow. It's a wifestyle of a unique kind.

Jesus must have felt keenly the sting of ingratitude and a lack of reinforcement. The very Son of God was vastly unappreciated. How many of us have been cursed and stripped and jeered at by bloodthirsty crowds, or derided publicly by kings. . .or crucified? Jesus' life was an arrow pointed in one direction. He chose the very best course and took the consequences that came with the territory.

Then there are our physical abilities. Few men could hold down two full-time jobs successfully and be a strong, godly parent and husband in the home, too. Yet women tend to expect this of themselves—and it's frankly unrealistic. One or the other must give ground. Which ground are you ready to give up? Your husband? Your children? Your church? Your community? Your job?

Many women have no choice but to work in addition to running a home. To them God says, "My grace is sufficient for you" (II Corinthians 12:9). If there is a choice, carefully and prayerfully choose your course together with your husband. Scripture invites us to trust in the Lord with all our hearts, not to lean on our own understanding of events and timetables (Proverbs 3:5-6). When we acknowledge God's total guidance over *all* the affairs and decisions of our homes, we can rejoice in the certainty of His guidance as we strike a clear path through a tangled world. He is the Good Shepherd of the sheep. We do well to listen to His voice and follow His direction. After all, it isn't hard to listen to someone who loves us, is it?

Biblical Principle:
  God promises to supply our needs.

My Scripture:
  "Let your way of life be free from the love of money,

111

being content with what you have; for He Himself has said, 'I will never desert you, nor will I ever forsake you'" (Hebrews 13:5).

My Prayer:
"How about it, Father? Do you want me to work? Let's talk about it. Or better yet, you do the talking and I'll listen. Show me what your will is. Help me to talk with my husband, to be sensitive to his feelings and leadership. I'll try to listen through all the noises of my world. I'm so glad you care about even this. Good Shepherd of my life, what would I do without you? Thank you for listening. Help me listen to you."

— 18 —
Balance Reclaimed

Play. . .rest. . .work. . . .Listen to the words. Let them form pictures in your mind. A child on a beach. A couple lying the in the sun. A laborer in the field.

How is it with you and your mate? Do you play together? Do you rest together? Do you work together or do you both work such long hours that play and rest, in their purest forms, have no meaning for you?

"My work *is* my play." You've heard it and so have I. And I understand what is meant. When the work you do is *that* good, you really do feel like it's play. There's true enjoyment in doing it.

Aside from work, however, what is play and rest to you? What part do they have in strengthening a marriage? Are there things you enjoy doing together? Apart?

Play and rest are essential and enjoyable parts of a balanced work life and a nourished marriage. Let's talk about them.

Work and Play

My writing desk this morning is my lap. My office is a cool summer porch with screens from ceiling to floor. Even as I write, I observe the work and play of the gold finches and squirrels. A major daily concern of my squirrel friends, and birds, too, seems to be food. The majority of their time is spent obtaining it, storing it, and eating it. That is how it should be—even in our lives.

Work is part of God's plan for all of us. It's not just something in the way of "real" ministry or "real" living, although it often seems so. It's good and right, and feeds and clothes us. It's also ministry, whether or not you ever verbally share your faith. But when the work is done. . .or even while it's going on, play and rest can and should occur.

The happiest people I know are able to mix these ingredients. They are able to forget work and throw themselves vigorously into play at times. And the opposite is also true. The Preacher of Ecclesiastes said, "Enjoy life with the woman whom you love all the days of your fleeting life which He has given to you under the sun; for this is your reward in life, and in your toil in which you have labored under the sun" (9:9).

My squirrels are a good example of mixing work and play. On their way to "lunch" yesterday, a playful trio chased each other all the way down a gigantic tree trunk in an arboreal ballet. It was almost symphonic. Twirling and spinning they went, in a furry frenzy of play and work. As they continued to eat their way through the woods, they kept it up. Circling up, circling down. Play, work. Work, play. No wonder they look so alert; seem so infinitely energetic. No wonder their round eyes sparkle. They aren't stressed out. They never will be. They *know* inside their little animal heads that God will provide for tomorrow. They put their energy for both work and play into today.

But we humans are so much smarter than they, aren't we? We're almost afraid to play, fearing there will be no provision for tomorrow. We think, in spite of what God Himself says, that if *our* resources run out (job, health, savings) God's will, too. Instead of living a more balanced and enjoyable life, how many of us race through our 20s and 30s under heavy, self-imposed burdens of work we don't need to bear, and then we hit bottom in mid-life or fall on the shores of the forties in complete exhaustion?

Our version of the Bible reads something like this: "*I will provide all my needs by working overtime, taking two jobs, etc. etc.*"

But the God of Scripture has something different in mind:

"My God will meet all your needs according to his glorious riches in Christ Jesus" (Philippians 4:19).

On the other hand, beautifully balancing and fleshing out the full scriptural truth, these verses tell us:

"Six days you shall labor. . ." (Exodus 34:21, NIV).

"If a man will not work, he shall not eat" (II Thessalonians 3:10).

Next comes the principle of rest in the same verse as the order to work:

". . .but on the seventh day *you shall rest; even during the plowing season and harvest* you must rest" (Exodus 34:21, NIV).

Even when there seems to be extreme necessity to work, we need *not* overwork, but to trust and rest. When working would mean ruining our bodies or our relationships, it's time to rest and trust, "even during harvest." This is not something you will read in success manuals or magazines. But then, why the sudden wave of classes and books on managing stress?

Can you hear the compassionate voice of God

ringing through His commands? Let's look at Ecclesiastes again. "...Exactly as a man is born, thus will he die. So, what is the advantage to him who toils for the wind? ...Here is what I have seen to be good and fitting: to eat, to drink and enjoy oneself in all one's labor in which he toils under the sun during the few years of his life which God has given him; for this is his reward" (5:16,18). He's simply telling us to be reasonable in our work. God's in charge. He has promised to provide for our *needs*. We, too often, are engrossed in supplying our wants. As a wise person once said, "He who is rich is he who has few needs."

In Scripture, God paints a picture for us of a balanced life of work, play, and rest. He dips His almighty brush in the well of earth-life and draws a life-sized picture of passionate splendor in sweeping strokes, alive with harmony and color...a life of balance and increasing peacefulness.

Work, rest. Rest, work. Play, rest. Rest, play, work. Like the hands of a grandfather clock. Rhythmic, regular, predictable, comfortable, reassuring, timeless. Work offsets play and play offsets work—takes the sharp edge off. Play and rest assure us we aren't slaves to our work and give us the motivation to go back to it with a better perspective.

I try to play a little every day, even if I only manage a short bike ride or a dip into a good book.

God set an example for us in the holy hush of dusk on the sixth day of creation. The earth and the people on it were finished. His explosion of creativity was complete.

"Thus the heavens and earth were complete in all their vast array."

By the sixth day, God had finished His work, and on the seventh day, He rested.

116

"And God blessed the seventh day and made it holy, because on it he rested from all the work of creating that he had done" (Genesis 2:1–3, NIV).

Can we ignore His example and not be the losers?

Look for a moment at the way our bodies were created. Normally, we must rest one third of each twenty-four hours in order to refuel. We really don't have a choice. Our bodies demand it. God could have made us otherwise. We could easily have been constructed to run twenty-four hours a day. Why weren't we? Sometimes I wonder if part of the reason wasn't to remind us once a day that we are dependent on God to renew us. In a strange sense, we are re-created each night as we rest in a death-like state. We are helpless and vulnerable. But in that quietness God restores our bodies and our spirits.

I happen to live in an area heavily populated by Dutch people. Because of their firm reverence for the Lord's Day, no stores were open on Sunday until just a few years ago. It would not have paid, because no one would have shopped! Now, there are a few, but they are brought in by chain market management with no feel for the values of the community. An uneasy pattern now edges its way into the pleasurable balanced living around us because some now *must* work on Sunday and others are lured to shop. The new and unpleasant cycle pushes rudely against an established order of work and rest which meshed well. For some, now, there is no more rest or day of worship.

God knew what He was doing when He established an order. It remains for you and me to uphold God's established order of work and rest in the marketplace of our lives and to exclude activities which prevent it. We have the substantial challenge of choosing to live God's way, by His example, or not living God's way.

We have the opportunity to live creatively, exhuber-antly in the last part of a century gone mad in so many ways. It's one of the many ways Christians can make a difference.

My little squirrel friend is sitting precariously on the jagged top of a broken tree. He is resting—taking time out to groom. First come the paws, then the tail. He's brisk and businesslike about his grooming, but he seems to enjoy it. Now he's resting. Now he's gone. That's you and me. Working, resting, gone.

I know without asking that most readers of this book will have a longing for "restedness." I hear it in my "marketplace." I see it in bloodshot eyes, sharp voices, and drooping eyelids. I see the invisible yokes worn by so many—ones they have put on themselves.

Whose yokes are you wearing, and what can you do about it?

Biblical Principle:

There is a time to work, a time to rest, and a time to play.

My Scripture:

"The man who fears God will avoid all extremes" (Ecclesiates 7:18b, NIV).

"Then I realized that it is good and proper for a man to eat and drink, and to find satisfaction in his toil-some labor under the sun during the few days of life God has given him—for this is his lot. Moreover, when God gives any man wealth and possessions, and enables him to enjoy them, to accept his lot and be happy in his work—this is a gift of God" (Ecclesiastes 5:18–19, NIV).

My Prayer:

"It sounds so good, this rest and play and work balance, Lord. But how can I make it work in my life? What shall I cut out and what shall I add? I think I'll just take a deep breath, right now, and listen for your presence. I'll remind myself that you hear the direction of my longings, and *you* will meet my need. Praise you!"

— 19 —
The River Of You

Woman, wife, mother, employee. So many of us punch three or more time clocks. Our days are lived out in a triangle of relationships that call for everything we can muster and then some.

Anne Morrow Lindbergh felt this when she wrote in *Gift From The Sea*, "Eternally, woman spills herself away in driblets to the thirsty, seldom being allowed the time, the quiet, the peace to let her pitcher fill up to the brim."

Compare this to a river. A river is always flowing, moving forward. But it is always being renewed at its source. If a river flowed without being renewed, it would soon become a creek, then a trickle, then a dry, cracked river bed capable of nourishing nothing and no one.

Your life and mine are rivers with tributaries to our children, our husbands, our jobs, our churches, our communities. But the river of you feeds your tributaries only to the extent your water source is replenished. If the river becomes stagnant, unrenewed, the tributaries you feed will tend to become the same way.

Again Anne Lindbergh says, "You need to learn how

to give with a purpose, but also how to renew your wellsprings of life." She urges (and wisely), "Don't try to water a field with a pitcher."

You cannot perpetually spill yourself away, either spiritually or physically, or you will see yourself go down the drain.

How then can you, the center of a revolving activity wheel of relationships, obligations, and activities, become that "still" axis? Let's talk about it.

Come Away. . .

If you feel "cornered" and stressed out, you really *need* to stand up and say, "Stop!" You *need* to find a time and place to be alone for one full day (at least). It's a biblical principle for which Jesus, John the Baptist, Paul, and many others in God's Word gave us the example long ago. This could be your own home or a friend's. It could be in a motel room, at a cottage, or on a long ride (without the kids). My favorite spot is a long stretch of beach along Lake Michigan where I spent a lot of time as a teenager. I choose an overcast, coldish day when nobody else would go there, and I walk.

After you have found a place, give yourself plenty of time to unwind. Hours if necessary. Walk. Jog. Sit in a hot fragrant bath with your favorite music playing. Cuddle up in an old bathrobe and sip a cup of steaming herbal tea (no stimulants like caffeine). Exercise. Unplug *all* phones and answer no doorbells.

Delight Yourself in the Lord. . .

When you've come to a place where you're ready, begin to open yourself to the Lord and His healing ministry in your life and spirit. Praise music may help you refocus your muddled thoughts. Visualize every word of the music. Try a few psalms of praise. Read them aloud. Try to use a full hour or two to listen to music, read God's Word, pray, and meditate. And finally, present yourself to Him for restoration of your body, mind, and soul.

When you pray, use *your* words, your way. Talk with Him as you would a friend who was sitting across from you in your living room. Tell Him everything on your heart. Ask for His guidance. Confess known sin. Accept forgiveness. You have come to The Source. You can drink deeply from the well that will never run dry.

Listen to the words of author Joyce Hefler from her book, *All Rivers Run To The Sea*: "We seem always off to one extreme or another, fearing relaxation will cause us to lose the race, when in fact it makes life new. It helps us wisely wait our turn. *Without relaxing we lose the race anyway.*"

Discern True Duty

Now you're ready to re-evaluate your busy life.

A. Get a notebook and pen.

B. Get comfortable.

C. Get excited! You're about to get a handle on this overload of yours.

D. Ready? Dig in.

First, list all your activities. (This means washing clothes, making beds, buying groceries, working at a paying job, watching television, cooking dinner, etc.)

On the next page, put the following headings. From the activities on your first page, choose the ones you *can't eliminate.*

ACTIVITIES I CAN'T ELIMINATE

ACTIVITY	WHY?	TIME IT TAKES	COULD ADJUST

Look at the X's in the last column. Even if you can't

eliminate some activities, you *can* adjust the time they take. You *do* have options!

Stay with me. Are you beginning to see the light at the end of the tunnel?

On a third page, list your activities from the first page under these headings:

ACTIVITIES I CAN CHANGE

ACTIVITY	HOW? (Delegate/Eliminate/Minimize)	WHEN
Ex: Den Mother	Eliminate	End of this term

The "When" column is your action column. You must make some tough decisions, and you must carry them out as soon as possible. Remember, "Without relaxing we've lost the race anyway."

Okay, you've got a handle on some of your over-involvement. Now, to *prevent* yourself from doing it again, try judging an activity by these criteria before you say "yes" to anything in the future.

1. Does my husband approve?
2. If I say "yes" to this, what other things will I have to say "no" to because of it?
3. Is it short-term or long-term?
4. Is it an emergency or an option?
5. Do I have a choice?
6. Have I prayed for God's direction?
7. Have I waited at least 24 hours before answering?
8. Does it violate the principles of Scripture in any way?
9. Will it enhance or detract from my marriage?
10. Will it dilute my time with God?
11. Will it really be a benefit to someone? To myself?
12. Is it already being done?

13. Am I spiritually gifted in this area?
14. Am I adequately trained or can I be?
15. Has God provided the physical strength?
16. Has God provided the time?
17. What is my motive in saying "yes"?
18. Do I want to do it? Am I enthusiastic about it?
19. *Do I have inner peace about my answer?*

If you do not have peace, reconsider. After I began using this list, I accepted a job which looked like a "yes" on most fronts—except the peace. Something in my spirit urged a strong caution which I ignored. I took the job and experienced sleepless nights, extreme stress, and near exhaustion. Eventually, I left the job, and my balance returned to normal. It had unbalanced my life unnecessarily.

Another time, another job looked good. But I had NO peace. At the last minute, after the interview which looked like a green light, I said "no." Peace rolled in like a river, and time proved the decision right.

Don't run on empty. Don't be afraid to take charge of your time involvements. Don't be afraid to trust God.

Biblical Principle:
A wise woman considers more than just her own desires or those of others when it comes to new involvements.

My Scripture:
"The wise woman builds her house, but the foolish tears it down with her own hands" (Proverbs 14:1, NASB).

My Prayer:

"Why, why, why, Lord, have I gotten myself into so much trouble with over-involvement? It seems like things are coming at me from all directions. Maybe this will help. Oh, Father, please be patient with me, give me wisdom as I sort it out. Thank you, again and again."

Part 4

This thing called love—it makes the world go 'round, puts the sun in sunshine, the joy in laughter—and demands nurture, care, protection. Of faith, hope, and love, the greatest is love.

— 20 —
Love Is . . .

"The discovery of another person is a sweet, almost ecstatic thing. The wonder of being able to talk with another far into the night. The surprise of a laugh, the odd sense of something being. . . found. Even on a porch swing."
—Walter Wangerin
As For Me And My House

As an introduction to this section, think about these definitions of *Love is. . .*

- "Keeping on" *through* the tough times—even when you would rather run away.
- Something we do by the grace of God.
- Walking through the valleys as well as climbing into the sunshine.
- What God does for us and what we can, in turn, do for others.
- Not an optional feature of marriage.
- Directing our hearts, our souls, our minds, our strength onto the loved one.
- Pulling our share of the load—and sometimes his when he isn't able.
- Having an orderly home (mostly!)
- Speaking up instead of clamming up when there

are words that need to be said.

- Something to be exercised, not buried.
- An avenue of pain and a highway of joy.
- Kind words in the face of anger or unjust criticism.
- Seeing him "off" when you've got "better" things to do.
- Caring enough about him to make yourself and your home an ornament for him.
- Listening to a subject you aren't interested in just because it interests him.
- Sacred and holy, not to be trampled upon.
- A constant discovery of the unique depths of the loved one.
- A hungry relationship, mysterious, possessing a soul.
- The ingredient in marriage that turns duty to joy.
- A promise to really care.
- A smile across a room full of people.
- A covenant between you and God to care.
- A spiritual, invisible circle in which two people may safely dwell.
- A deep red rose flourishing in spite of the weeds.

Now, add a few of your own.

LOVE IS:

-
-
-
-

My Scripture:
   "How is your beloved better than others, most beautiful of women?" (Song of Songs 5:9a, NIV).

130

— 21 —
Love And A Well-Ordered Home

It takes about twenty minutes to become a wife. . .or is it years?

Who among us holds a degree in "Wifing"? Where is the college that offers one? Or how about your adult education classes. Are there any night classes in "Wifery," or "Wifeing Skills," or maybe "Advanced Wifeing 301?" I haven't seen any, and don't think I will. Marriage is the only major contract we enter into with no preparation—no education—no guarantees.

Parenting is "in." Family living is "in." Seminars abound on every conceivable subject. Degrees can be earned in almost anything. But when we marry, most of us enter the sacred circle with only a few, one-hour pastoral counseling sessions at best and a bushel or more of lace-edged dreams.

But after the bouquet is tossed and it's time to change the sheets, dreams aren't enough. When you are pregnant and your husband has just lost his job, dreams alone won't make it. The stuff dreams are made of is gossamer, tinted a rosy shade of pink. When reality sinks in and the gossamer fades, every wife needs more than cotton candy dreams. She needs to know what it really takes to nurture and enjoy this marriage of hers. She needs to know what works and what doesn't.

Some wives get an informal kind of education from their childhood homes. Others do not. If your own mother set a good example for you, you are truly blessed, because home is where education for orderly "wifeing" begins. Unfortunately, too many of our homes today don't even offer this kind of "auditing" in the classroom of marriage.

School was in session every day of your childhood, though, whether it was intentional or not. Each event was a lesson in loving and living. If you saw your mother and father kiss heartily and often, you won't need anyone to tell you affection nurtures a marriage and that it's more than okay to smooch in front of the kids! If you weren't raised in a caring, well-ordered home, you may need a boost now and then to help you weave your dreams into the tapestry of marriage.

I was fortunate to grow up in a home where my parents loved each other, and we children knew it. They also loved us. This gave me security and a good example of how two married people ought to conduct themselves. Our home was clean and orderly and each of us knew what we could count on from the others in the home. My parents showed me by example the kind of symmetry that enriches a home.

My church also taught me to have an ordered spiritual life. Twice weekly (plus!) attendance in a solidly biblical church painted a clear picture of what God expected from husbands and wives, parents and kids.

All of these are rich resources, and I'm profoundly grateful they were a part of my experience. Through them, I came to believe and experience the truth that a well-ordered home contributes immeasurably to the happiness of the people tucked inside.

But where does this leave you? What kinds of "order" are most important for your home? And what is a "well-ordered" home?

Well-ordered does not mean perfect. There is no such "critter" as perfection this side of heaven. Nor does it mean spotless. The kind of effort exerted to have a spotless home can often have very negative results in a home. Well-ordered doesn't mean dictatorial or rigid, either. Dictatorships don't produce loving homes—the kind that can bend with the times and not break. Well-ordered, rather, means that a sense of prevailing balance and harmony is present a good share of the time. And when it isn't, the family members know its absence is just temporary. It means a husband can count on a number of things important to his life. It means wives and children can count on certain "givens." What kind of "givens" seem to be most important to husbands and wives? You'll have some of your own, but here are some, too. We'll expand on these thoughts in coming chapters.

Order Your Commitments

A husband has a right to count on *you*. One of the primary things a husband should always be able to count on is faithfulness—fidelity. If marriage means anything at all, it means two people have promised each other and God they will hold fast to each other until death separates them. Your husband should never have to worry about your commitment to him.

Our society calls it "cheating" or "having an affair" (whether emotional or physical). God calls it sin, and says you will suffer the loss of self-respect, the respect of others, power in your Christian life, and the death of love itself (Romans 7:2–3; I Corinthians 6:9–11,18–20).

Faithfulness is a key principle to an orderly wife life; it is foundational in all respects to a marriage that lasts.

Order Your Spirit

There are other aspects that need to be in order if married life is to flow, fresh and unsullied; if it is not to stagnate entirely. We need to order our spirits. That is, we must nourish and allow God to nourish our innermost beings so that out of us can flow a Christ-like spirit.

We can nourish our spirit in a number of ways: Beautiful music, inspirational reading, preaching, regular identification with other believers in church or small worship groups. We can be nourished by quiet times of private worship as we meditate on Scripture or godly music. We can carve out seasons of prayer (whole half-days at least once year). An ordered spirit is also foundational to an ordered marriage.

Order Your Priorities

Try to organize your life so about ninety percent of your time and energies go to meeting the needs of others and about ten percent go to meeting your own needs. If you think about it, most lives are already moving in that direction, only the ten percent is usually cut short because, "There's not enough time." Remember: you *need* that ten percent if you are to have anything left to give the other ninety percent of the time.

Ministering to others, whether at work, in the neighborhood, or in more formal ways has a mysterious, circular way of nourishing us while it nourishes others. It demands that we look outside the small circle we stand in, and touch the life of another in a meaningful way. Make a call. Deliver a plant. Jot a note. Pay a visit. Listen.

Inflow, outflow. Christ Himself often went to a solitary place to pray and meditate. His humanity demanded that he, too, refresh himself and fellowship with the Father in order to continue His ministry.

Nourish yourself. Nourish others. It's a good way to keep the river of you fresh and flowing. Take in, give out. This is the essence of the ordered spirit and ordered priorities.

Order Your Mind

The mind is a bottomless reservoir of information. We need to use discretion about the information we add to it. If you tend to be negative, associate with positive people. Avoid too many grisly newspaper accounts. Listen to uplifting radio and television programs. Exercise your mind muscles. Read. Keep a running list of books you want to read and choose a new subject of interest to focus on each year—something you know nothing about. Associate with others who challenge your thinking.

Dr. Bob Jones II, Chancellor and former President of Bob Jones University made a point to study thoroughly one new subject each year in order to broaden his understanding of people and events as well as to stimulate his mind muscles.

None of us needs to shut down the mind after graduation from high school or college. We don't need to be one of whom it is said, "She hasn't had a fresh thought in twenty years." If your opinions and attitudes *never* change and your practices *never* change, you are not growing as a person ought to grow. Actually, you are in imminent danger of becoming rigid, narrow, single-focused, and stubborn. Not only that, you may be more than a little dull.

Why put up with it? Walk to the windows of your mind and throw back the curtains. Open the shutters! Lift the sash and feel the cool breeze blow in, scattering dust and cobwebs everywhere.

Do you have a lot of questions about a subject? Write them down. Toss them in a folder. Research them in the library or by phone calls to people in the know. You could be in for a marvelous adventure.

Design your own college course in your *specific* area of interest and head for the library. It will cost you nothing but earn you everything.

If the emphasis on mind stretching seems to be off track as it relates to wife-life in the city, suburbs, or country, consider with me the value of interesting and informed conversation between couples.

If your husband could write your daily conversation script word for word, would it be substantially different from day to day? Would your conversation be sprinkled with well-worn opinions he has heard hundreds of times already? Would it contain the same old catch phrases and old jokes? Or would there be fresh, new insights and maybe some new questions to discuss?

If your husband already knows your script, there may be nothing left to discuss—and no need for conversation.

What do you know about the things which interest him most? What do you know about his work? If you know nothing about his interests, you really know very little about who he is.

My friend Brenda is taking a course in electricity because her husband is an electrician and she doesn't want his work to be a closed door between them. She's interested in him and, therefore, his work.

Order Your House

I have spent most of my life in Western Michigan, surrounded by well-ordered Dutch homes and home-makers (both men an women). Many of the women have entered the workplace as well, but they and their mates are able to manage a graceful lifestyle with less stress than some because they have learned to live well-ordered lives. They learned it from their parents. And we can learn it, too.

One of their philosophics goes something like this: "Make do or do without." They also believe cleanliness really is next to godliness. And, they believe in hard work and accountability to their homes and their community.

As a rule of thumb, they buy new and buy well. They maintain their purchases regularly and properly. They keep what they buy until it wears out (not just until it's out of style). I was impressed when I considered what this means in terms of years. It means less wages are needed because less is purchased. It means less shopping, less time devoted to acquiring, more time for other things. And that's just the beginning.

These people don't seem to be caught up in frantic acquisition, but, instead, they major on caring for a few, well-selected, functional items. Their windows gleam and their autos shine.

Cars are washed on Saturday so they are "ready for Sunday." Cookies are baked on Saturday in preparation for Sunday company after church. Lawns are faithfully mowed on Saturday so they, too, will be bright and shining for the Lord's Day. Dirt is attacked daily in organized fashion, so it never seems to accumulate and overwhelm them. Friday nights are often set aside as family nights to go somewhere or spend time with the kids. People know what to count on. Structure and order prevail, and there are many, many "givens." It is orderly, integrated, and secure. It's what we all need to some extent, and I believe we can have more of it. These kinds of homes tend to produce sound marriages. Is it any surprise?

So where do you start in ordering *your* home? It's probably best to start with the biggest "fire." Start with the place that needs order the most: the biggest mess—the dirtiest room—the most tangled schedule. It's a lot like fighting a fire when things are out of hand. You go for the biggest blaze and don't worry about the little embers until it's under control.

Let's use a common example of disorderliness: housekeeping. Poor housekeeping has fueled the fires of more than one divorce I know about. One woman who had crammed antiques in every nook of her home visited her newly estranged husband and found his walls *completely* empty of decoration. He simply couldn't take the clutter anymore. She had ignored his needs in a very important way.

Go ahead, tackle the big one. Then work your way down the list. Slowly. You can't do it all at once.

If housekeeping is your "Waterloo," what are your options?

1. Do it yourself.
2. Hire it done.
3. Delegate the chores.

If you do it yourself but are not a natural organizer, do what my friend Carol Currey did. She set up the file system of housekeeping suggested in *Sidetracked Home Executives* written by sisters Pam Young and Peggy Jones. It gave her the push she wanted.

Written from the "reformed slob" point-of-view, Pam Young writes, "I was a full-time homemaker, and my husband never knew when he'd get a meal or what he'd have to wear." Fourteen years and one divorce later, Pam concluded that: *"Everything* is affected by disorder."

Peggy also had a rocky road in her marriage due to disorder. She asked her husband in what order of importance would he put the following things:

1. A pretty, clean home.
2. Dinner on time.
3. A happy and contented wife.

His answer was beautiful: "I like to come in the back door and hear you singing. Then, I like to smell a good dinner, and finally, I notice how nice the house looks." He spoke giant words for mankind, for mankind appreciates them all, and usually in that order.

As we looked at some important components of an ordered home and marriage, did you find yourself saying "yes" to positive change and to the God who empowers you for change?

Biblical Principle:
Orderliness is important to God and therefore to us.

My Scripture:
"But let all things be done properly and in an orderly manner" (I Corinthians 14:40, NASB).

My Prayer:
"Here we go, Lord. I'm not sure I like the way this is starting out. Or even if I can handle it. If all of this is true, or even part of it, I need your help. . .now! Father, your universe is so orderly. Help me fashion my life, my marriage, my home after your example."

— 22 —
The Garden Of Your Love

Happy, healthy marriages don't grow on bushes (although we might wish it was that easy), and they aren't packaged and labeled, standing in neat rows on supermarket shelves. Wouldn't it be great if they were?

Actually, marriages need tending, much like a garden needs constant care and attention. Marriages also need love. But most of all, they need the Son.

In the garden of a good marriage, weeds need pulling all the time and nourishment must be constant, not just once in awhile. There are times to thin and times to prune and time to water. If a marriage is nourished well, it *will* grow from the life-source within it. It *will* blossom. It *will* bear fruit in other lives instead of being ingrown and obsessed with its own tribulations. There *will* be a harvest time. And it *will* be a sanctuary—a sacred circle of two.

How do things look in your garden? Is there wilt? Disease? Stunted growth perhaps? Or does it need more regular nourishment in order to flourish and bloom? Where do you begin?

Begin With God

Step back and take a good look at this husband God has planted in your life. Is he a diamond in the rough? Maybe he's a winner temporarily disguised as a loser. Is he unpolished? Perhaps. Unfinished? Certainly. Impossible? Never!

Begin, then, with an unswerving faith in our God of wonders who specializes in rough diamonds. He is the worker of miracles and the Almighty Sorter of tangled webs. Begin with Christ who offers daily grace and peace and power and abundant life to those who say "yes" in their hearts to who He is and what He came to do among us and within us.

My husband, your husband, impossible? Absolutely not. The song in your home may be ever so dim, discordant, even jarring. But we deal with a God who has been making melodies out of broken music boxes ever since Eden. If we are willing, God is ready.

Recognize The Rhythms

Sometimes, I think life is one, long calendar of seasons. We are all moving, changing, growing. Your husband today is not your husband of yesterday, or last month. You are married to a different person every month, every year. We find ourselves wanting to "freeze" those special moments that occur in relationships forever and forbid them to change. Yet, even while we are thinking about it, we are moving on in the flowing river of life, hurrying from eternity past to eternity future.

We are changing, too. In tune with the rhythms of life, our bodies, the times, in every way we are changing, mobile, alive. We cannot stay static. We can't remain twenty-five (or even thirty-nine) forever. New experiences and ideas—new information and new opportunities are all being fed into our lives, changing us and our mates. We each move onward, upward, slowly but surely toward the goal set for us by our heavenly Father: toward Christ-likeness and eternity.

Notice the rhythms God builds into the human experience. See how He steps back sometimes, giving us freedom to fall on our face, to grow and mature from it. He created the rhythms, and He works with them, not expecting adult Christian behavior from infants in Christ. He accepts us where we are, and lovingly urges us on toward maturity.

Now, turn around and notice the rhythms, the phases of growth in your husband. Youth. Middle-age. Mid-life crisis! Old age, sickness, and more. Each phase produces different joys and stresses as it pushes on to the next. Stop. Look. Listen to the "season" your loved one is in right now, today. Put what he says and does against his "seasonal" backdrop. Now you can understand. Now you know better what to expect and how to react and what to say. Now you've listened to his life rhythm. Now you're ready to move from understanding to nurturing. Now you're ready to encourage those weak notes into a hallelujah chorus instead of squashing the developing melody inside him.

We can't bind our husbands' growth so tightly that he has to fight to grow, like a blade of grass pushing up through hard clay—shoving, quarreling its way through the hardness toward the light. We need to urge, coax, encourage, facilitate. Because we want a relationship that "blossoms," we will notice the seasons and not try to harvest when it is still growing season.

We observe, we accept, we nourish. To push our husbands into the small box of "What he used to do," or "What I would do," or even, "Our church says," is to

142

bind him with ropes he may not be able to bear. It's to tempt him to snap the cords like a Samson in rebellion and run away. Some do.

"He lets me be me!" declared a wonderfully free and creative wife about her husband's actions toward her. And because this husband did, her life flowed out in a hundred delightful tributaries to those around her. He stood beside her, not in front. And I watched and learned the wisdom and the ways of letting go. He understood her eager, unfettered spirit and gave it outlets to grow.

How long it takes some of us to learn that the relationships we "free" are the ones that return to us most fully, with a distinct song of their own!

Christ sets us free to become complete in Him. We can set our husbands free to grow and become complete also.

"Get Them Through It"

A smiling Dr. James Dobson gave this tongue-in-cheek advice to parents on raising teens. He meant facilitate their growth and their change. And it's good advice for any wife moving through a significant change point with a husband. As we walk along beside him, we can remember the God who wisely and lovingly moves through our growing pains with us and beside us.

"Don't make mountains out of molehills!" grinned my petite Arkansas grandmother. And again she would say, "Consider the source." She wanted me to look at who people are and where they are coming from in their life experience. She wanted me to be smart enough not to turn what should be a skirmish into a full-scale war simply because I didn't understand the other person. With her pithy sayings, grandma urged

143

me to discern what was *worth* going to war over. As I remember Grandma Mary Ida, I try to remember the road my husband is traveling and apply her advice.

There are enough ripples and lots of waves for all marriages as we move through seasons of change, but as a wife uniquely gifted to be a creator of harmony, we need to recognize the rhythms and refuse to squelch the unfolding melody inside our husbands.

Break The Yokes

Who needs another yoke anyway? Look around you and see the spiritual bondages—the "thou shalt nots" that husbands and wives invent for each other. They write their own commandments. And when one "does" when he's supposed to "don't," the one who wrote the rule shudders in self-righteous robes of. . .murky gray.

God is altogether able to accomplish His work of conviction and instruction in righteousness in the life of our husbands without us playing God in his life. After all, it is the work of the *Holy Spirit* to convict him, not ours.

Often, our most significant contribution to the growth of our husbands is prayer for an open heart to God's wooing.

Let's loosen our grip and begin to celebrate our mates by setting each other free to grow and change. Let's be part of the harmony that gives depth and dimension and s p a c e to our relationship. And then we can lean back and enjoy the song now—and through all eternity.

Biblical Principle:
Let God be God.

144

My Scripture:
"Now the Lord is the Spirit; and where the Spirit of the Lord is, there is liberty. But we all, with unveiled face beholding as in a mirror the glory of the Lord, are being transformed into the same image from glory to glory, just as from the Lord, the Spirit" (II Corinthians 3:17-18).

"An excellent wife, who can find? . . .Strength and dignity are her clothing, and she smiles at the future" (Proverbs 31:10,25, NASB).

My Prayer:
"Lord, have I really been trying to do that? Trying in my own strength to do your job? How foolish I've been! Forgive me, Lord. I really am sorry. Help me let go of his spiritual development and just pray. I think I have a big problem in this area, Lord. Would you show me just what this means and how to "let go"? You know how much I want a truly spiritual home, a godly husband. I didn't mean to get in your way of accomplishing that."

— 23 —
The Gift Of Love

Let me tell a story on myself. It's a story I'd rather not remember. . .a story of expectations and about husbands and about wives.

It was December, and Christmas was just around the corner. Michigan was properly dressed in glistening white for the occasion. The stores were properly crowded and the streets properly slippery. Children were getting more and more impatient and adults shared secrets with conspiratorial smiles above children's heads. Country mailboxes were full of seasonal greetings, and it seemed easier to smile at strangers.

Our tree glistened in holiday splendor. Cookie smells filled the air. Presents were mounting under our tree daily. And Christmas seemed to have captured all of us in its special glow—all except my husband, that is. He was so busy with his work. No time for festivities or daydreaming beside the wood stove on cold nights. Maybe that's why there was no gift under the tree from him to me.

I had spent days shopping for gifts, and I had especially enjoyed buying his. Every time I glanced at his gaily wrapped box, I got a warm thrill of anticipation for Christmas Eve. I pictured the look on his face when he opened it and took great delight in it.

The holiday drew nearer, and still no gift from my husband lay under the tree. (Yes, I kept looking!) That one thing flawed my joy, and I let that one thing grow until it almost sent our Christmas careening into oblivion.

I began to give myself explanations for the lack of a gift, beginning with, "He's too busy to shop." I began to watch his comings and goings (yes, I did!) to see if he was sneaking in a little surprise shopping trip and hoping it was so. But all his time was neatly accounted for, and I was surprised I couldn't seem to let this go. I consoled myself by imagining he was building something special out in the barn when I couldn't see him. Then, two days before Christmas, I frankly wondered if he was going to take time to remember his wife at all. Feathers began to ruffle, and the father of lies got his foot in the door. "See", he said, "he really doesn't think much of you or he would _____."
Satan filled in the blank.

These thoughts affected my attitude which, in turn, affected the Christmas atmosphere around our house. I began asking the kids if they knew of any gift their dad was hiding from me, my insecurity growing. The whole thing was entirely out of proportion to its importance by now. I wanted a gift from him in the worst way. I wanted him to reciprocate my love gift in my way.

By Christmas Eve, my emotions were chasing each other in tight, heated circles. We were to open our gifts, and still there was nothing from Roy to me. I caught him looking at me strangely a couple of times but couldn't interpret the look. The Christmas tree winked, but I didn't wink back. I was trying, unsuccessfully, not to hurt, but the bruises were showing. And there was a small part of me that wanted them to show.

After the Christmas Eve meal and dishes, darkness had set in. We pushed in a plug, and the tree blazed and twinkled with Christmas delight. Gifts were passed out amid much merriment and squeals of surprised glee. My gifts from the children were warming. But they weren't enough. We each opened one gift at a time until everything under the tree had disappeared.

Suddenly, an envelope appeared out of nowhere and was dropped on my lap by a smiling husband. My cheeks burned as I opened it and discovered coupons for dinners for two, nights out at a Civic theater. . .and tucked in the back was a check toward a new typewriter of my choosing. I was utterly abashed and ashamed about my suspicions. He had *known* all along that I thought I was forgotten and that was the worst of it all.

There was a tense moment, but tears, smiles, apologies and laughter melted together as the moment passed. His gift was so personal and so much what I had wanted. He had given it in his own way in his own time. I had put him in a box of my expectations. . .and suffered for it. How wrong! I realized that night that I needed to completely free my husband from the bondage of finding and fulfilling my expectations. I needed to appreciate him exactly as he was and enjoy his "male" approach to things. I needed to learn both how to be abased and how to abound. And, I needed to learn how to glory in even imagined tribulation.

That night, darkness fell in a velvet cape around us. The children went to bed. Heat danced in waves above the wood stove, and stars pushed their way through a Christmas Eve sky, decorating it for all the world to see. Moonlight reflected peacefully off white snowbanks. And Christmas had arrived in our hearts once more.

Biblical Principle:
Practice contentment in every situation.

My Scripture:
"Do not be anxious about anything, but in everything, by prayer and petition, with thanksgiving, present your requests to God. And the peace of God, which transcends all understanding, will guard your hearts and your minds in Christ Jesus." (Philippians 4:6-7, NIV)

My Prayer
"Dear Lord, here are my expectations for my husband. You know them all; I wrote them in my heart. But I give them all up to you. There are so many things I wish he would do for me and with me. I don't think he even knows the half of them. It's a pretty long list, isn't it? Help me, Lord. Help me not to waste time and energy on what he doesn't do, but to be honestly grateful for what he is and what he does do. I'll need your constant help, Lord. I get blinded pretty easily. Forgive me, Lord, and help me turn loose of these expectations that could eventually grow into a wall between us."

— 24 —
One Is The Number Of Love

You were a radiant bride! You stood there, a graceful nymph filled with the rosy bloom of life. Remember the day? Remember the white magnificence of your gown. . .the awful case of nerves? Remember your vows, the electricity of the moment and the surge of eager, joyous commitment to the trembling man at your side? Remember the music leapfrogging ahead of you down the aisle when you were introduced to your friends as "Mr. and Mrs." for the first time? The two of you stood in the center of the universe; the earth was your footstool, and all creation gave you a standing ovation. *He* was your earthly number one!

How is it today? How is it now? Is your husband still a VIP in your life? Or has he descended the ladder of importance and become not much more than a wage-earning spectator coming in last on every front? Maybe he falls somewhere in between the cracks of your life. And maybe, just maybe, you haven't even thought about it.

When you pledged your life and love to *him*, did you have a hidden clause that read "until the kids come along?" Or "until I have my own career?" Or did it just happen? Maybe it's in the process of happening right now.

Stop right here and reflect for a few minutes. How is it between you and your husband these days? Don't focus on his pluses or minuses, just ask yourself, "Is _____ really important to me?" "Do I let him know it?" Sounds incredibly outdated, doesn't it? Either that, or it sounds astonishingly and radically new. Him? Important? What about *ME*? There! Now we're on more familiar ground. What about *my* rights? Now we're really talking!

I'm afraid that even as Christian wives *WE HAVE ALLOWED OURSELVES TO BECOME SECULARIZED!* We look and act exactly like wives who never heard of Jesus Christ and His radical message of salvation. We have allowed the media, in every shape and form, to structure our thinking and attitudes instead of God's Word. If we even *begin* to nurture someone else more than ourselves, our inner computers flash a warning "stop." And marriages are crumbling in frightened little piles all around us. Something is off base, isn't it?

What does work, then? Let's look at three Christian marriages, which followed, unwittingly, the suggestions and patterns of the secularized, Christ-less world system:

(1) Susan and Bill had decided to send their three young children to a Christian school, but Bill's wages couldn't cover the cost. Their solution? Put Mary to work outside the home as well as inside. Mary desperately wanted to be home with the children. Yet, she was torn between wanting the best possible schooling for them and her husband's obvious willingness to have her pay the bill. Besides, all of their friends and

151

relatives were doing it this way. Suddenly, Mary and Bill didn't see each other anymore because their hours conflicted. Suddenly, their family was split into times "Mom was home" and times "Dad was home." They touched only in passing. Suddenly, when mom *was* home, she was overcome by house maintenance and child care. Suddenly, there was barely time to worship the Lord she loved and no time to serve Him in ways she was gifted. Suddenly, their marriage was writhing in silent agony which more than occasionally spilled out on their children and their friends.

This couple put their children before their marriage and had to experience the resulting agony until such time as they could hear God whisper, "Your marriage, then your children."

(2) Shirley sacrificed everything for her large family of children and her husband. The kids had music lessons and opportunities of every sort. They sang in churches and were well-known in their city and beyond. They attended the best colleges and earned degrees. And Shirley was absorbed in it all. But over the years. . . back at home. . .the marriage was crumbling and torn. The husband was a shadow—an unheralded, virtually unnoticed wage-earner who was slowly being starved of reinforcement, respect, and love. He began to lash out at his wife, both physically and emotionally, feeling driven by his unmet needs—feeling cornered and cheated. Shirley, too, had sacrificed her marriage on the altar of her children without realizing it. And in the midst of all the lessons, perhaps the most important one was overlooked: *How To Properly Nourish A Marriage.* And now, the children are gone, and nothing is left for either marriage partner.

In the middle of it all, this determined Christian mother was convinced she was doing right. She couldn't imagine why her "awful," "hateful" husband was such an unhappy man, and she became even more complaining and demanding in his presence.

These are true accounts with the names changed, of course. But if we put spiritual truth into action, we can see how God meant their homes to be.

These couples were putting the children's interests before their marrige in such a way that it continuously robbed their marriage of any joy and fulfillment it could have had. It didn't work, and it won't work, because it isn't God's plan for the home. God did not mean that children should receive love and attention and time and money *to the exclusion of the marriage relationship.*

Any family can live through some occasional "bumpy times" when special and even prolonged attention must be given the children to the exclusion of the parents' time for each other. During these times, what makes the difference is that both know it's *temporary,* and they are *anxious* to be together again, to enjoy one another as soon as possible. But when it doesn't seem to make a difference, and when the pattern of neglect continues, on purpose, it begins to rot the core of marital happiness. And this is also true if it's the husband who neglects the relationship.

(3) Carol was a mother through and through. She was born to be a mother, and she gave it 100 percent. But, she couldn't ever seem to be away from the children—not even to travel on short trips with her husband. She worried about the children the entire time she was away. At home, the husband often fixed his own meals and felt selfish because he wished she would. And the love between them began to mildew, and mold set in, and counseling was needed.

God took this couple and, as they surrendered to

153

Him, His Spirit gently pried open their hearts, and she began to nurture his needs, too. Her children began their schooling in Marriage 101. This sincere Christian wife began setting an alarm clock across the room to make herself get up early enough to fix her husband's breakfast so she could share a quiet moment with him. And their boat stopped rocking, and the counseling wasn't needed any more. And the children learned, before it was too late, what it was to nurture a marriage.

As you read, you may shake your head, thinking your children will be or will feel neglected if you give more thought and care to their dad. You may be afraid they can't grow up properly without all the time and money they receive right now. But isn't that a lack of trust? Don't we have a God who always takes care of the details when we obey Him? Isn't it true that the *results* of obedience are not our business, but obedience is?

Of course I'm not advocating immediate, radical, or foolish moves to neglect your children. I am, however, urging you to rediscover how to respect and venerate and love your husband increasingly. . .better today than yesterday.

I'd like to suggest that the greatest possible gift we can give our children is to thoroughly *love* our husbands. Nurture his emotional needs. Enjoy him. Laugh with him. *Be* with him. Hug him. Hold hands with him. Flirt with him in the presence of the kids. Cooperate with him. Discuss with him. Ask for his opinion. Pray with him (but don't nag him into praying!). Worship with him. This kind of active loving is like sending our kids to a 20-year college on marital happiness. They will be well-prepared for their own marriages as a result.

If you have "front-row kids" and a "back-row

husband," run to God and tell Him. Confess your inability to even want a change. But tell Him you are willing to be made willing. He meets us there, you know—at the trysting place at the foot of the cross where eternal exchanges are made forever, and where holy fire enters jars of clay, transforming the hopeless into the invincible! I know. I've been there.

Biblical Principle:
To respect, honor, and love my husband above any other human relationship for Christ's sake.

My Scripture:
"Wives, submit to your husbands as to the Lord." (Ephesians 5:22, NIV)
"...The wife must respect her husband." (Ephesians 5:33b, NIV)
"If you have any encouragement from being united with Christ, if any comfort from his love, if any fellowship with the Spirit, if any tenderness and compassion, then make my joy complete by being like-minded, having the same love, being one in spirit and purpose" (Philippians 2:1-2, NIV).

My Prayer:
"Lord, I don't want to do this. My kids mean everything to me. They nourish me and fulfill me. I enjoy meeting their needs. But this seems really important, so please make it important to me. Make me want to nourish and love my husband like I do my children. No, He's not number one in our family. I'm sorry, but he's not. And I had no idea. Father God, I stand here, open-handed and really quite ashamed. Take this crumbly marriage, consume the dross with your holy

fire, and scatter the ugly ashes as far as the east is from the west. I've sinned, Lord, against you and against him. Forgive me, and help me start again. Not with fanfares, but with a quiet spirit of obedience to you and joy."

— 25 —
Love Is Air In The Tires

Actually, when the alarm doesn't go off and the oatmeal burns, I lose interest in keeping on. That is *not* a good way to start a day. But it is real—it happens. And that's because wife-life at the grass roots can deliver a lot of surprises. Like my newlywed years when I spent my days changing (cloth) diapers, cleaning (you-wax) floors, cooking (without a microwave), and keeping up with three super-charged bodies. Yes. . . a lot of surprises.

In my mind, I was doing everything a wife ought to do, and expected praise for it—at least occasionally. And occasionally it came, after the right amount of hinting. But most of the praise came when I did something that was really important TO HIM.

True Love would leave in the morning and throw an afterthought my way such as, "Could you put some air in the tires today, Hon?" Sure. I could do that. And fifteen diapers later it was time for dinner, and I had forgotten. Air in the tires went in one ear and out the other. *I* wasn't in the least interested in car maintenance. But it was a mistake to assume *he* wasn't.

157

Four-thirty would roll around and no air had been put in the tires. Actually, it was last on my list of priorities.

True Love would return and look around with glazed eyes at sparkling house, gourmet meals, smiling kids and ask, "Did you put air in the tires, Hon?" Hon hadn't. *And this happened more than once before I caught on!* Things like this had to happen a lot of times before I realized a powerful principle: WHAT MATTERS TO HIM HAD BETTER MATTER TO ME. He would have been contented with peanut butter sandwiches—if only the tires had air in them. The floors need not shine and the kids need not smile—if only there is air in the tires. In the course of time, I began to learn to do the things that mattered most to my husband early in the day, *before* I got sidetracked.

The other things I did mattered. Oh yes. But this was just the maleness in him asking for attention to one or two other matters I would normally ignore.

Today, twenty-eight years later, I put up the screen door *before* I took myself out to lunch and began writing. Why? The flies bothered him all last evening, and tonight he would ask first of all, "Did you find time to get the screen door up, Hon?"

God has made woman an able helper to man, his counterpart. If a husband senses his needs are important to his wife, it meets a deep need inside him, and becomes a bonding between mates. The act itself is not as important as the *desire* he senses to make living pleasant for him.

Philosophies of the world *en garde!* Here comes Jesus with an altogether new formula for success: Lose yourself. Love others in the same way Christ loves us: Unreservedly, unconditionally, self-sacrificingly. Seek first the happiness of others. Pour yourself out as a fragrant offering. Cast your bread upon the waters. Do unto others as you want them to do to you. Give and it shall be given. Look on the needs of others.

Ah, dear Lord! I have tried you and not found you wanting.

Christ-like love speaks volumes to any husband. When he has a wife he can count on to be concerned about what touches him, servant love brings a surprise of joy into marriage. There is a hidden secret of sorts wrapped up in it, and ideally, both partners will search for ways to enhance the life of the other, to be servants to one another.

When any one of us senses we are truly loved by another, the sun seems to shine a little bit brighter. Not only that, but it produces within the loved one a desire to respond positively in the relationship.

Biblical Principle:
To be alert to the needs of other people in much the same way we're aware of our own needs.

My Scripture:
"Each of you should look not only to your own interests, but also to the interests of others" (Philippians 2:4, NIV).

My Prayer:
"Dear God, how can I be as selfish as I am so much of the time! I am, Lord, forgive me. I am really wrapped up in my own 'stuff' and 'things' and plans. Lord, show me today the special things that will mean a lot to _____. I'll give it a try, by your grace. Help me look at his interests from *your* perspective of our marriage."

— 26 —
Love Is Peanut Butter

Marriage is a beautiful, seamless garment made of lace and leather. God Himself made two, unique, puzzle-piece people who match each other. Woman and man. Each strong. Each weak. Each made to offset and counterbalance the other. A perfect match in God's economy. "One flesh," God called them in Genesis 2:24. A delighted Adam may well have looked at his new wife and commented, "Bone of my bone! Flesh of my flesh!" But that was just the first of many surprises as they lived out their lives together—the seamless garment.

Both are so different—like needle and thread, soap and water. Just like day and night are different but intricately related. Even the differences in both can bring a delight to the union. Especially if we are on the lookout for little ways to bring a smile to the other.

The virtuous woman outlined for us in Proverbs 31 "brings him [her husband] *good*, not harm, all the days of her life" (31:12, NIV). And we can do the same thing, because God makes us able. . .and gives us the "want to." The Lord God said to the woman, "Your desire will be for your husband" (Genesis 3:16, NIV).

So how *can* you bring a little surprise of joy to your husband now and then? Where's the starting line?

Most of us love to do things for others that we want done for us. You might begin by discovering (or *remembering* if you have forgotten) what *he* likes.

Example: My daughter recently packed a romantic picnic basket for herself and her date. Crystal glasses were lovingly tucked in between rose-covered, linen napkins. She arranged tiny cheeses and sausages artistically on a glass dish. Gourmet delicacies nestled happily in the surprised basket so used to styrofoam cups and paper plates. A tablecloth draped in folds from under the cover of the basket. It was a delight to the feminine eye. But the boyfriend? Well, he was very male—very into sports. A man's man. So who was the basket for? You guessed it. Of course he loved it, because it represented time and effort and caring. *That's* what *he* liked. It was an altogether special picnic, yet it was a female expression of her own desires, too.

Then, experiment! You may be able to introduce your husband (and he, you) to new delights and to discover new vistas together. For some men, simply having their wife *enjoy* one of their pleasures with them is a treat. Go ahead, *try* fishing. *Try* golfing. *Try* new foods. One wife I know avoided trying golf for many years. But after the first game, she became an avid fan. From that point on, she and her husband took golfing vacations!

If your relationship is already on keel, small attentions will feed the fires of affection. If yours is not a good marriage, it is possible that even small steps may lead to a new beginning. Remember to have that bill paid or that tire balanced. Remember that pepper makes him sick. Remember how awful he feels in blue and what memories he would rather not discuss. Remember how he loves a cup of tea after dinner, and how he likes it fixed.

In my home, peanut butter is king, and its presence in the cabinet means, "I love you." The whole kitchen may be bursting with foodstuffs, but if there is no peanut butter, then there is no food around. In a strange sort of way, peanut butter is love.

You know what they are—those little attentions to detail that make up "the seamless garment" of marriage. You discovered several of them during your courtship. You've probably learned more since. Pick from the bouquet of them and surprise him with some little pleasures that can mean everything.

The object in all this is not to see how much you can spoil your husband, but to exhibit a holy kind of love in ways he will understand and appreciate.

One wife I know tucks little love notes in unexpected places for her beloved. She's 75-years-old and much adored and respected by her well-loved husband. Another woman pulls the plug on the phones, lowers the lights, and sets out a gourmet delight for just the two of them when the time is right. She's nearing 70 years of age. One wife waits up for her preacher husband (no matter how late) after deacon board meetings with a favorite snack and a little back rub. Each of these marriages is solid, unshakable, and full of tender love and laughter. Each of these wives know what *their* husbands appreciate. Because these wives are continually nurturing their mates, that nurturing brings a like response from their husbands. The marriages are healthy and minister in a thousand ways in many other lives.

Husbands! They can be so very male in their attempts to be loving! Appreciate it! Smile at it! Enjoy it! You married a *man*.

On one of our anniversaries my darling Roy announced his intention of buying me a manual can opener (seriously!) to his office staff. The girls were properly horrified, while the men thought it was a fair idea—as good as any they could come up with. The can opener *did* have a 5-year guarantee, and it was sturdy. It would last (which meant a lot to him), and it was unromantic (which meant a lot to me!)

When he handed me the box and I unwrapped it, I looked at him and grinned my thanks. I *knew* this man. And I loved him and his gift. How could I be petulant when I knew his motives? How could I feel cheated when it was given in love?

Respect the masculinity of some gifts and roll with the punches. He's trying his level best to say, "I love you." He's trying to please you! He feels faint and awkward in a lingerie deparment, so buy your own, and love the guy who brings the can openers of your life. You'll never be sorry. And neither will he.

Biblical Principle:
Look past the obvious act to the motive of the giver, and give credit where credit is due.

My Scripture:
"Above all, love each other deeply because love covers over a multitude of sins" (I Peter 4:8, NIV).

My Prayer:
"Oh, dear Father, these men you have made are so funny sometimes. Mine's practical when I want him to be romantic, and romantic when I need him to be practical. Lord, when my husband brings "can-openers" to me, help me to see love written all over them, and not to throw the gift back at him—or to grin until he has left the room!"

— 27 —
Love Unties His Gifts

If your husband is a Christian, if he has placed his life under the wings of the Almighty, he possesses one or more spiritual gifts. And, just in case this is a new concept to you, a spiritual gift is a gift (or gifts) from the Holy Spirit to each believer. It is a motivation and an enablement to do God's work.

God determines *who* gets *what* gift (I Corinthians 12:7–11; Ephesians 4:11–13). And there is a splendid, dazzling array of them.

Whatever the spiritual gift, there is only one reason for having it—to "serve others" (I Peter 4:10, NIV), and for one purpose, "so that in all things God may be praised through Jesus Christ" (I Peter 4:11). They are given "for the common good" (I Corinthians 12:7).

My husband, for example, shows strong evidence of having the gifts of serving and giving. They are a beautiful combinaton and blend perfectly with his whole personality. Whenever a ministry is in need of funds or hands-on help, his heart *and* pocketbook respond immediately. Mine remain unmoved.

My gifts are entirely different, but I stand in awe at the way God gives gifts of the Spirit which complement the rest of who we are. Only He could make such a blended whole.

When someone is in need, my husband wants to give money and practical help, as I've mentioned. My first response is to rush in with profound sympathy and compassion and do a lot of listening.

Someone else might invite them to dinner (hospitality), or give needed advice about changing their situation (wisdom, knowledge). Some would lift them in a powerful wave of intercession. Each individual in the body of Christ is enabled to minister to the whole person in need.

As each of us moves closer to the heart of the Lord, we become more responsive, more moldable, more useful in ministry to others. And as we free each other to minister in our colorful kaleidoscope of ways, the hurting world is touched by the great I Am who Himself lives in us and yearns to minister to them through us.

Can you see the value of allowing your husband to express his spiritual gifts? Can you begin to understand how you could quench the Holy Spirit by refusing to allow him expression? Can you grasp the consequences of muzzling these good gifts of God?

I have a good friend, a dedicated Christian, who understands and works well with this concept of freeing her husband's gifts. Dave is gifted with hospitality, for instance, and it is one of his first responses to any situation. Pat's gift is not hospitality, but she wisely allows Dave to minister and grows by hostessing as many groups as she reasonably can. She *is* gifted with exceptional faith which is exerted in a daily prayer time averaging two hours. She is also burdened to spread the "good news" of Jesus Christ and serves actively in Christian Women's Clubs. Dave frees her to do this rather than take a paid job. He encourages her participation in small group prayer and worship sessions also, and God *moves* through Pat's prayers in awesome ways. Her recorded answers to prayer yearly number in the hundreds.

Recently my husband asked me, "What color wood stove shall we buy?" He added, "The black one is $300 cheaper." Taking a baby step into the new stewardship God is pressing me into I said (to his surprise), "Let's get the black one, and that way we can give the $300 to someone who needs it." He was delighted, and within two days the Lord had shown him who needed it.

God is waiting—*waiting* for each of us to liberate our gifts and those of our mates. I believe He longs to use us to minister to those around us and that *we* hold back showers of blessing by quenching the Spirit in each other.

The word "Christian" means "little Christs." Think of it! We are "little Christs" to our world. To the neighbor we don't like, to the co-worker we're angry with, to the husband we live with. Dare we put a stopper on each other and chain the Holy Spirit of God?

How do we bind the Spirit? By saying "no" when your husband's heart says "yes." By standing in his way when he wants to go forward. By criticizing instead of praising. By resisting instead of cooperating.

But what if your husband gives too much money to God's work? Won't you be in danger of going without? I guess the first question is, "What's *too much*?" Yes, I think I can safely say you *will* be in danger of going without extras and comforts and pleasures so some others can have necessities. But what kind of imitation Christianity do we have which only gives when it promises not to hurt? Only when we don't have to sacrifice? Only when we don't take any risks?

Jesus gave all. . .*all*. . .ALL! And it hurt him unbearably. Christianity is not about *getting*, about hoarding and accumulating and storing. It's about opening our storehouses and our barns and our freezers and sharing out of our abundance, even out of our want. *This* is what our cynical world is standing on tiptoe to see. *This* is witnessing.

Maybe you don't know your husband's spiritual gift—or yours. Ask yourself, quite simply, what are you both motivated to do for Christ? Write your answer(s) in here:

Me: _____

Him: _____

Now, do it! Somehow, some way, do it. Free your husband to be a man of God. Don't hold him back or stunt his growth because you are afraid or because you are unwilling to cooperate. Tear off those binding chains of fear and doubt and toss them back in the face of Satan who has been whispering these things into our ears ever since Eden.

It's time to dare! To trust! To *believe!* To fly in the face of fear and doubt and soar on the wings of faith.

Untie his gifts. . .AND SOAR!

Biblical Principle:
Don't be a stumbling block; be a steppingstone.

My Scripture:
"So then, men ought to regard us as servants of Christ and as those entrusted with the secret things of God. Now it is required that those who have been given a trust must prove faithful" (I Corinthians 4:1-2, NIV).

"Therefore let us stop passing judgment on one

another. Instead, make up your mind not to put any stumbling block or obstacle in your brother's way" (Romans 14:13, NIV).

My Prayer:
"Okay, Lord. Here he is, gifts and all. Full steam ahead. Forgive me. . .again. I didn't realize what I was doing. Use my husband to minister like you want him to, only I'll leave it up to you to keep him in balance. It's kind of scary, Lord. Do you know what I mean? But you know what you're doing. Of that, I'm sure. Oh, by the way, would you help me to use your gifts wisely, too? Help me be your vessel of service so that you are glorified."

— 28 —
When Romance Flickers

It was just yesterday. . . .

My boyfriend and I had just broken up, through the mail, again! I was a very disconsolate college girl 1,000 miles from home, and positive I had seen the last of him. Suddenly and surely, I knew that *not* seeing him was *not* what I wanted. As I sat on my bunk, chin in hand, staring at nothing, a soft knock tapped at my dorm door and a male voice questioned, "Linda, Linda Palmer?" I hurried to open the door and found myself eye to eye with a delivery man holding an armload of what looked like one million red roses.

"For you," he smiled, pushing the fragrant mass into my hands. I looked at the tucked-away card and read, "I love you. Roy." Blood drained from my head, and I edged my way faintly back to the bunk. Red roses. I love you. It wasn't over then! Of course! He'd realized it, too. We *did* love each other. Why not stop this foolishness and get married? And so we did, twenty-eight years ago. It was a lace-edged, sparkling moment of romantic delirium.

Do you sometimes find yourself longing for candle-light and roses? Wouldn't you enjoy a really romantic

169

approach once in awhile from your funny, maddening logic-dominated husband who just *can't* quite seem to understand what it is you want?

What Is It Really?

Let's talk about romantic love. Not from a psychologist's point-of-view or a theologian's corner, but woman-to-woman, as we feel it and understand it and *want* it.

We women, we wives, have a whole compartment in us that enjoys rose-colored moments and flower gardens and kisses blown across a crowded room and holding hands in church. We like light, loving touches that turn our emotions ever so slightly to "simmer." We love caresses that make no demands but show affection. We love affection. Affection makes us loving. It's a merry-go-round of joy.

Affection *is* a very real part of romance—her twin sister. They go hand in hand. Affectionate romance is our time to receive and give undemanding love—the kind that says softly, "You're wonderful. Stand back and let me look at you. Let me love you with my eyes."

Our womanly nature responds to sensitive consideration and tender touches and sweet surprises that talk louder than words. But we're woman, and *we* know that. If only "they" knew our secrets.

The kind of romance that satisfies us most can be felt across a room without a touch or a word. In the eyes of a husband, it can convey a velvet message to our spirits.

The Way We Like It

Because we're women, we enjoy being adored, nurtured. Somehow, I think, buried under all the dusty business of our days, we all know it. We are designed to enjoy being lovingly and genuinely noticed.

I know a woman executive who is *all* business. Yet she was profoundly touched when treated with tasteful, mannerly, affectionate reserve and appreciation by a (rare) *gentleman* who made her feel like a woman. Coming from a husband, this is what we call dynamite!

What we really seem to like most about romance is the feeling of being very special, sought after, attractive. It's part of the creative scheme of things, and it's certainly all right to enjoy it fully *when it comes*, which may or may not be often. God planned for us to enjoy marriage. He really did.

The Song of Solomon is a rapturous melody glowing with romantic love at its height. It is an ideal picture of the joys God planned to be experienced by married (and only married) couples.

But the way *we* need romance is probably *not* the way we will always receive it from our very mortal husbands. Let's talk about why.

To begin with, because he's a man, your husband will probably not have a strong personal need for or understanding of romantic love—the kind that touches the senses. That's because his primary love needs lean more to the physical expression than to the emotional or spiritual aspect of love. He is tempted to bypass the "flirtation" aspect of loving mainly because he *doesn't understand* the romantic nature of you, his wife, *and* because his primary need *is* physical. There are mysterious "rivers of you" he will not *naturally* understand unless told.

When your husband does not give you the romantic love you crave, it is not necessarily because he's a boor (although that *may* be true!). It's not necessarily because he's insensitive. It's because, in part at least, he's a man with *different sensitivities* than yours. Different. A most important word to remember. Just as a kitten is not "better" or "worse" than an elephant, man is not "better" or "worse;" he's *different*. And you did marry him for better. . .or for worse.

The Way We Receive It

Have you ever tried to demand romance? What happened? You know, we really cannot badger someone into romance (or love). This very tactic will shrivel romance before it flowers and is a sure way to drive a wedge between any two people. Men will run away from a "puller" or a "demander," in spirit if not bodily (behind the newspaper? in front of the television?).

If your husband is romantic, appreciate it! Don't do like a woman I know who continually ignored the orchids her husband brought her—until they stopped coming. Or the wife who said "stop" to the perfume he loved to bring. He stopped, but he didn't know how to express his romantic feelings any other way, so they stopped, too. A wife can either shut off the male-tinted moves toward romance or keep the channels open. Sometimes. . .romance is what you allow it to become.

If there is *no* romance, or bumbling efforts only, all is not lost! Really! Life *can* be lived, and very successfully, even if you *never* get a flower or an undemanding kiss. This may simply be one of the unchangeables you must live without.

But then again. . .maybe you could. . .

Rekindle the Embers

Dr. Ed Wheat, author of *Intended For Pleasure*, writes, "The greatest desire of love is to find an answering love. There is nothing that can so quickly build or rebuild the intense feeling of love in marriage than repeatedly reaching out to a responding partner.

"Romance can ignite (or *re*-ignite) at any time within a marriage. It doesn't have to be confined to the courtship and honeymoon. These are special times, framed in silver frames, but romance doesn't have to stop there and in happy marriages, it doesn't."

Romance from a husband is generally a "triggered" response brought out in him by our femininity. Not many husbands can produce romance at will *in spite of* the way we are. It's hard to hug a screamer or a nagger or a demander. Romance cannot be dragged out of a man. When romance comes, it should be a surprise of joy—a gift from him to you, made all the more special by its rarity and received with love.

Husbands respond, sometimes romantically, when they feel loved and respected. Our challenge is: Can we find ways to show these two vital self-esteem boosters? To develop them? Our inborn inclination to nurture will help as we ask ourselves a few questions:

(1) Just how does my husband enjoy being nurtured?

My own feels nurtured when I prepare and bring him a cup of herbal tea with a cookie on the side. Simple act. Profound message. Most feel special when their opinion is sought, or their accomplishments are sincerely praised. But these acts should not be "scenes" used to squeeze out romance like toothpaste or to manipulate. If you can't honestly praise or notice him in these ways, wait until you can, or find others. Most of all, ask God to open your eyes. You may blinded to the real man inside your husband's skin.

(2) Has the romance died in me?

(3) Do I admire him the way I used to?

(4) Do I enjoy him, respect him, flirt with him?

(5) Do I dress for him when I can?

(6) Do I dab on his favorite perfume for "special moments"?

Remember that romance is a two-way street. In most ordinary circumstances, romance can be encouraged by your loving actions toward him.

Remember? Romance from a husband is a triggered response to our femininity. Help him respond.

Help Him Respond

God gave special words of direction to the church at Ephesus in the book of Revelation (chapter 2). This church had lost their first love for Christ. God told them simply and plainly: "Do the things you did at first" (2:5b, NIV). The people in the church had grown cold and old in the love relationship. Icebergs prevailed. They had done some commendable, good things, but *they had stopped spending time with the Lord.* They had stopped *talking* and *communicating* with Him in prayer. They had ceased to be *exciting and warmed in His holy presence.*

Have you stopped doing the things you did during your dating and engagement days? Has the love grown "chilly," distant? Romance begins and ends with being with the loved one however you can. Phone calls, letters, dates, taped messages, quick lunches, lingering dinners, early mornings, late evenings.

Doing again the things, thoughts, and feelings of the first flush of love is a rich concept from the heart of God. . .a directive for rekindling the kind of love that keeps unfolding like a fresh rosebud.

Doing Without

Because we live in a sin-tainted, un-idealistic world,

we must look at the very real possibility that we may need to become content in the circle of marriage minus a lot of romance.

There are flip-flop seasons of marriage, for instance, when children seem to demand all our time and energy, or when over-involvement robs us of the time to even listen to the voice of our inner needs.

As an older man looking back, King Solomon wisely wrote, "There is a time for everything. . .a time to embrace and a time to refrain." We don't demand or expect the roses in our gardens to be in full bloom twelve months out of the year. Blooms are seasonal and, realistically, so is romance. For the rose, there is the season of rest (winter) and the season of awakening (spring). There is the season of budding and growth. And then, there is the brief time of full bloom for which we have waited. It doesn't last forever, but it will come again if nurtured properly. Romance will do the same.

A true rose gardener will never say the full-blown rose isn't worth the wait. He won't impatiently tie plastic roses on the stems and pretend either. I've yet to see a gardener brood angrily as the green bud, pregnant with flower, slowly expands, swelling and mounding in perfect syncopation with its nature. No, the gardener waits in joy for the birth of the rose, no matter how long it takes. The gardener, the one who planted the seed and nourished it, waits, excited about the first buds, and the promise of beauty and fragrance they hold. He was the one who gave it the nourishment it needed when it needed it and pulled the weeds that would have spoiled the bloom. He is the one who has lavished the most care and attention, who feels the most joy and pride when the rose blooms, and who then lovingly praises the beauty of the bloom to all who will listen.

Wives are the gardeners of romance. We must prepare the soil in our gardens. Pull out the weeds. Plant the seeds. And move through the various stages of waiting with anticipation.

If your rose never fully blooms, or doesn't bloom often enough to suit you, you can still manage your garden well and faithfully. And, without even realizing it, you will become, in the process, a fragrant rose yourself. . .but God will know.

Biblical Principle:
Life has its ebb and flow, ups and downs. It is not static or trouble-free.

My Scripture:
"My lover spoke and said to me, 'Arise, my darling, my beautiful one, and come with me. See! The winter is past; the rains are over and gone. . .the season of singing has come' " (Song of Songs 2:10-12, NIV).

My Prayer:
"Father, help me to enjoy fully the times of romance—and help me to be patient and realistic when life gets practical. Help me be a better gardener, tending gently, carefully, consistently the garden in which you have planted me."

Your Name Is Joseph!

The beautiful young wife and mother sat across the living room from me, black eyebrows arched into question marks.

"What should I do?" she asked.

An old boyfriend had been calling, someone she had nearly loved before her marriage. He called when her husband was away, which was often. He showed up at her door and told her she was attractive and that he needed her—his marriage was floundering. She had a counselor's heart and listened. She has a woman's heart—and was oddly moved at the attention and compliments. She also had a Christian's heart and had counseled with scores of teenagers in her community.

"He's gone so much," she said of her husband. He shouldn't have been.

"And it all seems so innocent." It wasn't, no matter what the reason.

Her memory was beeping signals of longing to her, and she was listening.

She *was* attractive. She was vital and healthy and young. Her husband *was* busy, and she *was* vulnerable.

Enter father of lies, dangling the dangerous beauty of the rose-colored past in front of her. Enter Accuser of the Brethren, suggesting she was no longer romanced enough at home and could invite it from other sources. Enter Angel of Light in glittering disguise, standing beside an open door to "fulfillment."

Her defenses were down. The timing was right for the attack. She wore no armor of God and had already been hit between the shoulder blades. She was seriously wounded but not yet a fallen soldier. Satan is not an idiot.

"What shall I do?"

"Run!"

"But it's so innocent."

"No it's not. Resist!"

"But it's so good to feel attractive."

"Pray!"

"What good would it do?"

She said she would listen. But she didn't. Maybe because the arrow was imbedded too deeply already, and she really didn't want it pulled out.

Divorce. When I heard the news, it was a dagger in my heart. The noise of the shattered home reverberated in endless circles throughout the community of believers and unbelievers alike, bringing sorrow and disappointment.

The story which had begun with loneliness and temptation would not end for many, many years to come because the book of marriage, once opened, is never really closed. The binding is only torn.

Another time, another woman sat across from me in a restaurant. She, too, was attractive and married. She, too, was vulnerable even though committed to staying in a marriage that didn't satisfy and probably never would.

She saw "the other man" at work every day. Inappropriate messages were delivered via eyes and words.

He was single, good looking, available, and drawn to her.

"Is it my imagination?"

"Probably not."

"It seems so good to be noticed this way even though it makes me feel dirty somehow."

"Temptation always seems good."

"Is there any real harm?"

"All the harm in the world."

"Would it hurt anybody?"

"Everybody."

"We're kindred spirits."

"That's not even relevant."

"What shall I do?"

"Run!"

"How?"

"As fast as you can, as far as you can, as quick as you can."

"What else?"

"Resist!"

"How?"

"Submit yourself to God, resist the devil, and he will flee from you."

"Then what?"

"Pray."

"How?"

"Lead me not into temptation but deliver me from evil."

"When?"

"Immediately."

The blue eyes were all anxiousness, all turmoil. She wrestled with temptation, acknowledged it, fought it scripturally, and won.

So what's a wife to do when another man starts to look good? What happens when she realizes she's being drawn toward unfaithfulness?

What's she to do when the home front is cool and it looks so warm in "the house next door"?

God gave us Joseph for times like these. Remember Joseph's predicament in Genesis 39? He was fully trusted to run his master's household and left in charge when the master traveled.

Then it happened. The master's wife got tired of her husband's constant business trips and decided to entertain herself with handsome Joseph. After all, he was young and well-muscled.

"Come!" she invited. "The master is gone. Come to my bed."

Joseph, at the peak of his manhood and unmarried, *must* have felt the full emotional impact of the temptation. He was not a eunuch.

Not content to be rebuffed once, the master's wife tried to seduce Joseph time after time as he went about his household duties. She talked cunningly and smoothly. Then one day she grabbed his arm and *as he pulled away,* she was left standing with his coat and her wounded pride.

Look closer at this scenario. Joseph couldn't leave town. He was a slave, albeit a highly trusted one, but he had no means to exist on his own.

He could not physically leave, but he did what he could and did it well. He ran from her pressure. He resisted. He undoubtedly prayed.

Oh, Joseph, you speak so loudly! We hear the voices of your actions calling to us over the ramparts of centuries telling us it *is* entirely possible to resist temptation. It *is* entirely possible to live purely and faithfully. You show us how. You lead the way. You hold the lantern for our path.

It isn't a sin to be tempted. The Lord was tempted as

we are, yet did not sin (Hebrews 4:15). It is, however, a sin to give in to the temptation. It's not a shame to be attacked—that's to be expected. It is a shame and a sin to open the door, put out the welcome mat, and invite temptation back the *second time.* God's Word tells us, "No temptation has seized you except what is common to man. And God is faithful; he will not let you be tempted beyond what you can bear. But when you are tempted, he will also provide a way out so that you can stand up under it" (I Corinthians 10:13, NIV).

Unfaithfulness. It's sucking the life and blood from homes all over America. But it's only a symptom of hearts starved for a deep relationship with God and looking elsewhere for something, *anything* that satisfies. A new "love affair" will never fill our God-shaped emptiness. Never! We may try to push and maneuver and force it to fit, but it won't.

Remember King David of Israel? He was beloved of God, yet he gave in to his sensual appetites and committed adultery with another man's wife. We can learn a lot from this godly man who still fell deep into sin (II Samuel 11; 23:8–13).

David was handsome. He was rich. He was famous. David, of the ruddy complexion and charcoal hair and dancing eyes and poetic heart. Songwriter par excellance. Creator of the hymnbook used in Solomon's Temple for congregational worship. A commander/king who skillfully managed 12 units of militia with 24,000 men in each. Warrior David, hero of his fighting professionals: the 600 mighty men and the 30 heroes. Literary marvel, this king. National hero, he. Lover of God. Commanding. Responsive. Courageous. Marvelous. But this fearless, mighty King David. . .didn't resist.

At a time in his middle years, probably when he was

181

most susceptible, Satan led the attack with the help of the demon "lust."

David had it all, including two beautiful, intelligent wives and several concubines (legal wives). He was the reigning hero of Israel with a briefcase bulging with success stories and a resume that crackled.

So what really happened?

The perfume of spring misted the air of Israel. Animals and humans alike stretched in happy abandon in the golden sun of the day and relaxed in the early evening of the warmer days.

It was also the time when kings go to war. Winter was over. But this time King David had not gone to war with his contemporaries. Instead, he had sent General Joab out with his men. Perhaps he was "feeling his age." Jerusalem beckoned. He had gone to war enough. Yet prolonged leisure wasn't his style, not for a man like him.

One evening he arose from his couch and pushed strong feet into sandals. He strode uneasily around the flat palace roof, deep in thought. Perhaps words of a new song formed in his mind as he walked, hands behind his back. The quiet of evening brought with it the sound of water splashing.

His natural curiosity was aroused, and David followed the sounds to a place where he could see a courtyard below the palace and a woman bathing herself.

David could not take his eyes from her. She was beautiful and young, probably totally unaware that she could be seen from above her bathing enclosure. He sent his messenger to find out about her. "Isn't this Bathsheba, the daughter of Eliam and the wife of Uriah the Hittite?" the servant asked (II Samuel 11:3).

David sent more messengers and had Bathsheba brought to him at the palace. There, the adultery was consummated, and Bathsheba was with child by the King of Israel.

Trapped by his own uncontrollable passion, a now fearful David tried to cover his tracks and ended up engineering her husband's death.

David married Bathsheba and she bore him a child, but the son died in infancy. David pled with the Lord for the child's life, but sin bears heavy consequences. Caught, remorseful, even repentant, sin bore its penalty because ". . .by doing this you have made the enemies of the Lord show utter contempt" (II Samuel 12:14, NIV). "Be not deceived; God is not mocked: for whatsoever a man soweth, that shall he also reap" (Galatians 6:7, KJV).

"But each one is tempted when, by his own evil desire, he is dragged away and enticed. Then, after desire has conceived, it gives birth to sin; and sin, when it is full grown, gives birth to death" (James 1:14, NIV).

There was a natural progression to David's sin. And this matters to you and me because we are brother and sister to David. We can fall in the same way he did. Note how it happened:

1. Leisure time unproductively filled. Not being in the place he should have been.
2. Enticed by the lust of the eyes and of the flesh. Turning to sensual pleasure not rightfully his.
3. Desire opens the door to enjoyment of the temptation.
4. Sin occurs.
5. Death ensues for Uriah *and* the illegitimate baby.

If David had run, resisted, and prayed immediately

after he saw Bathsheba, we would not have this story in Scripture. If he had caught himself early, and wrestled the sin to the ground by approaching the King of heaven, power would have been his. Two lives, a woman's purity, and the sanctity of a marriage would have been preserved.

Dr. Larry Crabb, writing in *Inside Out* says, "When people turn from God, the first thing they pursue when God removes His restraining hand is sexual pleasure."

The command for the foundation for a holy marriage is clear, ". . .Submit yourselves, then, to God" (James 4:7, NIV). . .

. . .the God of love,
. . .the God who abhors sin,
. . .the God who desires our fellowship,
. . .the God who makes us overcomers,
. . .the God who gives joy.

Biblical Principle:
We can overcome temptation to sin by submitting ourselves to God and resisting Satan.

My Scripture:
"A wife of noble character is her husband's crown, but a disgraceful wife is like decay in his bones. . . .No harm befalls the righteous, but the wicked have their fill of trouble" (Proverbs 12:4,21, NIV).

"Let marriage be held in honor among all, and let the marriage bed be undefiled; for fornicators and adulterers God will judge" (Hebrews 13:4).

My Prayer:
"Father, I see how Satan can blind me until I'm in an

awful state. Right now, this very moment, I ask you to bind all the powers of darkness set on destroying my life and my marriage. You promised that the name of the Lord is my strong tower. I can run to it and be safe. Father, I'm doing that now. Apply all your mighty strength against the forces set on evil in my life. I beg for your mercy, your enabling, and your protection. I seek complete deliverance from all such temptations and the grace to be consistent in living for you. Father, sometimes my thoughts wander into areas they shouldn't. Forgive me. Deliver me from the temptation. Close forever Satan's access to my mind through the gate of lust. Thank you. . .in the name of Jesus."

— 30 —
In Conclusion. . .

*"The man/woman relationship is a marvelous crea-
tion, wrought of many, tiny irregular pieces. Real life is
like that—wondrous and disorderly."*
Elizabeth Cody Newenhuyse
"A Glowing and Intricate Mosaic"
Marriage Partnership, Spring 1988

We've come to the end of our journey, you and I.
We've done lots of talking and thinking about being a
wife. Hopefully, we've grown into a fuller understanding
of what it means to be a Christian and married in
today's society. We've looked into the Bible and discovered a God who yearns over us like a mother hen
over her baby chicks and has provided guiding principles for every situation. We have gathered the wondrous knowledge that there are, indeed, plainly stated
biblical principles for marriage. God does care. He
does instruct. He does reward obedience. He does
allow us to bear the consequences of our disobedience.
He "parents" us—lovingly and perfectly.

Some of the areas discussed may have hit home.
Others could be skimmed past because they were not a
problem. The idea has been to improve our "wifeman-

ship." to be a wife whose marriage sings and keeps its melody, rightly understanding how to honor, preserve, and protect that ultimate earthly commitment.

Now it's time to pause and take a deep breath before putting this book down. Now it's time to reflect on how much you can expect from yourself, and how much you can expect from God as you walk forward into your tomorrows.

What To Expect From Yourself

Generally, *u sudden burst of energy* directed toward being a better wife immediately follows putting down a book of this nature. That's good! It signals a responsive heart, and Scripture reminds us that God honors a "broken and contrite heart" (a responsive one) (Psalm 51:17).

Also, *a lot of creative juices* may be bubbling, simmering, ready to take off in a tailor-made direction for your marriage. That's great! Our wise God has given us principles as well as rigid rules. He allows us to move freely and creatively under the umbrella of His one authoritative Book, the Bible. For example, the Scripture, "Love one another. As I have loved you, so you must love one another" (John 14;34) leaves the *method* of loving up to us. We are creatures of great liberty and choice and expression.

A third response may be *discouragement*. You may think, "I can't do all that." That's okay. The thoughts, suggestions, and principles between the covers of this book have been learned and experienced *one at a time* over a period of years. They have only one purpose: to show that obedience to God's guidelines for living and loving always result in a fuller, stronger life. When *we* obey, *He* goes to work. When we surrender, believe, obey—on a daily basis—we can confidently leave the outworking of those actions to God. It's *His* reputation at stake!

There's one last thing we can expect from ourselves, and that is *failure*. We may try very hard to apply some of these ideas and fall flat. But that's okay as long as we can laugh at ourself, get up, dust ourself off, and try again, trusting God to educate us along the way. Gold medals are never won by athletes who quit the first time they fail. Babies would never learn to walk if they never tried a second time.

Marriage is a garden, and we are growing every day. We are blossoming in ways we don't even realize. And God says that His strength is made perfect in our weaknesses. Each day, in new ways, we will learn how strong He is and how much we need Him.

What To Expect From God

Let's talk about *who* God is before we talk about what to expect from Him.

Character is who we are under the skin. Character is who God is through and through. The God of Scripture reveals Himself to be:

1. Everywhere present at once.
2. Full of *all* knowledge, about everything.
3. Power itself.
4. Love personified.
5. The beginning and the end of all things.
6. Everlasting, yet with no beginning and no end.
7. Good. . .very good.
8. Holy. . .without sin.

And this is only the beginning. . .only a taste of God. Psalm 104 gives us some idea of the praise due God.

1. He is clothed with splendor and majesty, wrapped in light.
2. The clouds are His chariot, and He rides on the

wings of the wind.
3. The wind is His messenger, fire His servant.
4. He set the earth on its foundations, gave boundaries to the oceans, lakes, and streams.
5. He gives and takes away life.

We deal with a God who is a BIG God. A merciful God. A God who loves. Only good comes from Him. He is our source of life, love, and salvation. He extends to us the gifts of eternal life and forgiveness of sin. We can only begin to see Him as he is, but there is enough to assure us that He is powerful and that He keeps His promises.

He is also a God of truth. We can expect Him to be faithful and true. We can know that He expects truth from us. And if we do not see Him this way, we do not know Him well enough yet.

A two-year-old child doesn't think his mother is wise and loving when she forbids him to play in the poison ivy. He thinks she's a spoilsport! She's out to get him! Just as he is not mature enough to understand her fully, we cannot fully understand God (I Corinthians 13:12). But what we do know inspires awe and bends our knees in worship.

Irresistible wifestyles—a simple, exhausting, exasperating, joyful journey in God's school of marriage. Listen to His voice. . .His heartbeat, His instructions. Know that He is beside you and in you, around you and underneath you even when you don't feel His presence.

Your husband is waiting.

The First Love Letter

My Darling Adam,

I catch my breath at how our spirits agree. . .at how we seem to understand so much of each other without words. I see our brand new love song as two separate melodies, sung in harmony, composed in the music room of heaven.

Our love is the kiss of sunshine. . .a gift from the heart of our God. It's laughter in all the right places . . .a forever song that will sound so much better sung together.

Thank you, my newly beloved, for delighting in my coming. . .for enjoying the differences in us. You make my journey so much easier. Thank you, too, for sometimes stepping back and letting me try wings alone. . .and for praying as this caterpillar becomes a butterfly.

We're both travelers down roads we've never seen. . . tasting new flavors. . .meeting new challenges. . . climbing new mountains. . .and doing it better because of each other. . .and because of our loving, gracious Father God.

I try to count the treasures of this new life—but there are so many! Cradling them like glistening jewels, I take particular satisfaction in the splendid riches of your love. . .and all the joys that lie ahead of us.

Your new wife,
Eve